single. dating. engaged. married.

navigating the four critical seasons of relationship

STUDY GUIDE | SIX SESSIONS

ben stuart

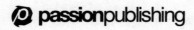 passionpublishing

W PUBLISHING GROUP

AN IMPRINT OF THOMAS NELSON

Published in Nashville, Tennessee, by W Publishing Group, an imprint of Thomas Nelson. W Publishing Group and Thomas Nelson are registered trademarks of HarperCollins Christian Publishing, Inc.

All Scripture quotations, unless otherwise noted, are from the Christian Standard Bible®, copyright © 2017 by Holman Bible Publishers. Used by permission. Christian Standard Bible® and CSB® are federally registered trademarks of Holman Bible Publishers.

Scripture quotations marked NIV are taken from The Holy Bible, New International Version®, NIV®. Copyright © 1973, 1978, 1984, 2011 by Biblica, Inc.™ Used by permission. All rights reserved worldwide.

Scripture quotations marked NLT are taken from the Holy Bible, New Living Translation, copyright © 1996, 2004, 2015 by Tyndale House Foundation. Used by permission of Tyndale House Publishers, Inc., Carol Stream, Illinois 60188. All rights reserved.

Scripture quotations marked NASB are taken from the NEW AMERICAN STANDARD BIBLE®, Copyright © 1960, 1962, 1963, 1968, 1971, 1972, 1973, 1975, 1977, 1995 by The Lockman Foundation. Used by permission.

This study was originally published under the title *Life + Love* by LifeWay Press® (ISBN 978-1-5359-6555-2). Editorial team includes: Ben Reed, *writer*; Joel Polk, *editorial team leader*; Reid Patton, *content editor*; Brian Daniel, *manager, short-term discipleship*; David Haney, *production editor*; Michael Kelley, *director, discipleship & groups ministry*; and Jon Rodda, *art director*.

Published in partnership with Passion Publishing, LLC

Thomas Nelson titles may be purchased in bulk for educational, business, fundraising, or sales promotional use. For information, please e-mail SpecialMarkets@ThomasNelson.com.

ISBN 978-0-310-14004-7 (softcover)

ISBN 978-0-310-1-4005-4 (ebook)

First Printing February 2021 / Printed in the United States of America

contents

introduction

People can endure almost any *what* if they have a compelling *why*.

If you think about some of the most heroic, inspirational actions of human beings in history, they usually took place because a compelling reason prompted a momentous action. A soldier leaped on a grenade, sacrificing his own life, because of his love for his friends. A mother singlehandedly lifted a car because her great love for her child trapped underneath the vehicle recruited an otherworldly level of adrenaline from her body. It's incredible what has happened because of inspirational *whys*.

Why mention this?

As we talk about our relational seasons—singleness, dating, engagement, and marriage—I want you to embrace the realization that God has given us a specific, compelling reason for each of these stages. When we understand this reason, we're equipped to engage every moment of our day in that season with a tremendous sense of purpose. Eternal significance can touch down on every mundane moment. And I want you to live a life like that.

I don't want you just to survive singleness. I want you to fulfill every God-given purpose for your single stage so that if it ends, you'll know you didn't waste a second of it. Even the most mundane tasks were shot through with meaning because you knew the compelling, God-ordained *why* behind the *what* of being single.

The same goes for dating. I want you to be amazing at it. I want you to journey through dating with a clear view of that unique season's purpose. And I want you to link hands with someone special and run through the stages of engagement and marriage together with a singular, compelling vision for your joined lives.

I don't want you to settle for just existing in whatever season of life you're in. Whether you're single, dating, engaged, or married I don't want you to lock your gaze on the minimum you have to do in life just to skate by and pass the time. I want you to live every season of your life to the hilt. I want you to crush it. I want you to be as successful as humanly possible while experiencing the unique opportunities and challenges that accompany each relational stage.

The good news: you don't have to try to create the meaning of each stage. God has done that for you. You can wake up every day, regardless of what stage you're in, and embrace the moments before you with a deeply motivated sense of meaning.

In the pages ahead and with the videos we'll watch together, we'll take a look at the purposes God has established for each relational stage you'll journey through. And the purposes of the stages relate to and inform one another. So whatever stage you're in, clarity is present for you in each category. I'm excited to run this race with you, and I'm cheering you on every step of the way!

Ben Stuart

about the author

Ben Stuart is the pastor of Passion City Church in Washington, D.C. Previously, Ben served for eleven years as the Executive Director of Breakaway Ministries, a weekly Bible study attended by thousands of college students on the campus of Texas A&M. Ben earned a master's degree in historical theology from Dallas Theological Seminary. Ben and his wife, Donna, live to inspire and equip people to walk with God for a lifetime. They live in the District with their three kids, Hannah, Sparrow, and Owen.

Ben is the author of *Single, Dating, Engaged, Married: Navigating Life and Love in the Modern Age* and the Bible study *This Changes Everything*.

how to use this study

This Bible study provides a guided process for individuals and small groups to think biblically about human relationships. Six sessions of study examine four different stages of relationships: singleness, dating, engagement, and marriage.

group study

Regardless of what day of the week your group meets, each session of content begins with the group session. Each group session uses the following format to facilitate simple yet meaningful interaction among group members and with God's Word.

start

The group session will begin with a few questions designed to help you introduce the session's topic of study and encourage everyone to engage with the study.

this session's topic

This section provides context for understanding how the session's topic is viewed in our broader culture. From here you will transition to the video teaching from Pastor Ben Stuart.

watch

Key statements and Scripture verses from the video session are provided so that group members can follow along as they watch the video teaching.

discuss

This section is the main component of the group session. The questions provided are designed to facilitate the group study of the session's topic. The goal is to better understand biblical teaching on one of the four relationship stages.

personal study

Three days of personal study are provided after each group session to help individuals think biblically about the session's topic. With biblical teaching and introspective questions, these lessons challenge individuals to grow in their understanding of God's Word and to respond in faith and obedience.

biblical case study

The first section of personal study considers the session's topic from the perspective of a biblical character. The Bible is filled with stories of real people who grappled with many of the same issues we deal with today. We have much to glean from their examples.

personal application

The next section of personal study takes what members have learned in the case study and seeks to apply the teaching at the heart level. These questions and activities are more introspective and personal than those provided in the previous section. Members should give time and consideration to their answers.

journal

The personal-study section ends with a journaling activity designed to help members tie together all they've studied during the week.

leader guide

A leader's guide for each session is provided on pages 128–42, which highlights key points from each session and offers helpful considerations for leading a group discussion.

session one

singleness

group study

start

Welcome to session one.

Begin this study by introducing yourself to the group. As we start our journey together through this Bible study, we find ourselves at different stages. Some of us are single and want to be. Others are dating and wish we weren't. Others hope to be engaged soon. Some are married. Take a moment and share with the group the life stage you're in.

What's your current relationship status, and how long have you *> intro*
been in this season of life?

What about this season brings you joy? What frustrates you? *> group a*

Each season provides unique challenges, frustrations, and joys. Let's begin by asking ourselves two introspective questions:

1. Am I moving toward becoming content where I am?

> *I have learned to be content in whatever circumstances I find myself.*
> **PHILIPPIANS 4:11**

2. Am I honoring God in every area of my life in the unique season in which I find myself?

> *I am able to do all things through him who strengthens me.*
> **PHILIPPIANS 4:13**

With these two questions in mind, let's get started.

this session's topic

Use this section to provide necessary context for the session's topic.

read

Though seasons of singleness vary in length, God has purposed that every human being on the planet experience this stage of life. So it's fair to ask the question: Why? If we say the purpose of singleness is simply to find someone to marry, then we're saying Jesus and the apostle Paul failed at singleness. I don't know anyone who wants to say that. So let's ask the fair question: What does God want our single season to be about?

Pray together; then begin video session one.

watch

Use these statements to follow along as you watch video session one.

You are most free when you fulfill God's created intent for your life.

The purpose of singleness is to pursue an undistracted devotion to the Lord.

You're not just made by God; you're made for God.

We're meant to get really good at being near God, to hear His heartbeat, to know what He cares about, to be attentive to His Word and His work.

Flourishing under God

1. You need to <u>know</u> <u>Him.</u>

2. Be attentive to <u>His</u> <u>work.</u>

People like to be around (life-giving people.)

discuss

Use these questions to discuss the video teaching.

We're at our best when we function as we were designed. Freedom isn't the absence of boundaries. It's the ability to fulfill our created intent. Fish are most free when they swim, and birds when they fly. The same is true of human beings. We're most alive when we fulfill our Creator's intent for our lives.

Kelsey

Read 1 Corinthians 7:32,35. Why did Paul say God has ordained a season of singleness for every person?

If singleness existed just to lead us to marriage, Jesus was a failure.

Singleness offers freedom that married life doesn't. How does devotion to the Lord look different during a season of singleness?

In what ways would marriage detract from your freedom?

Because of the freedom single people experience, they have more time to focus. However, most people use this season to focus on one of two interests:

1. CAREER. They're working to get ahead or climb the ladder.

2. THEMSELVES. They say things like "I'm taking this time to focus on me."

Neither of these pursuits is wrong, and yet neither focus will ultimately satisfy our hearts.

What pursuit, other than Jesus, are you tempted to focus on because of the freedom found in the phase of singleness?

Ben told the story of Jesus talking with the woman at the well in John 4:1-26. Jesus encountered a woman who had been married five times and was now living with a man. He told the woman her problem was that she was thirsty for something only the Lord could satisfy. We have to get our relationship with God right before we can ever hope to get a relationship with a guy or a girl right.

Have you seen this thirst in people who were looking to satisfy themselves with something only the Lord can satisfy? What does an unhealthy thirst look like in the context of a relationship?

By contrast, what does it look like to thirst for the purposes and priorities of the Lord?

In Greek the word *devotion* is made up of two words: *good* and *beside,* meaning we need to become good at being beside God, attentive to His Word and involved in His work. Ben gave some practical ways we can do this, from reading and writing out the Gospels to making extra money to sponsor a child.

What changes can you make in the way you structure your time in order to prioritize devotion to God? What do you need to uproot from your schedule and plant in your life so that you can focus on devotion to God?

What can you do this week to take advantage of your freedom as a single person that you won't have as a married person?

If you're not single, how might this discussion be helpful to single people you know?

prayer

Close the session with prayer.

Ask God to help the group treasure Him during the stage of singleness. Pray for patience when you're tempted to rush through this stage and for help to center your lives in Him alone so that you can grow spiritually before joining your lives with someone else. Ask Him to help you find rest in Jesus.

[handwritten: Kelsey]

[handwritten:]
- Patience
- Trust
- Center lives on God
- Rest in Jesus

[handwritten:] ★ take a group picture

personal study

paul // biblical case study

mission

Sometimes the best way to figure out how to do something is to watch someone else do it. There's a reason the Internet is filled with how-to videos. Often it's easier to show than to tell. This same principle applies to navigating singleness. What we really need is a good example. We need someone we can look to who lived the single life well.

The Bible doesn't let us down. The apostle Paul was an extraordinary example for us. He even said, "Imitate me, as I also imitate Christ" (1 Corinthians 11:1). The final portion of his letter to his young protégé Timothy, written from prison, shows us what a single life lived well looks like. Paul gives us a vision of what our single years, when lived to the glory of God, can be and accomplish.

Read 2 Timothy 4:9-12.

This passage may sound strange, and we may be tempted to skip over these hard-to-pronounce names because we don't know who they were. But Paul is showing us that even from a prison cell, close to his death, he was directing ministry. Make the decision now that nothing in life will keep you from fulfilling the purposes God has assigned to you. Your mission isn't complete until God calls you home.

In this passage Paul, at the end of his life, was talking about the people he had invested in who would carry the torch of the gospel after he was gone. Notice that Paul's ministry strategy involved mentoring young people who, in turn, would use their lives to help others. Second Timothy 2, just a few chapters earlier, shows that investing in the next generation was a pattern for Paul and a highlight of his life.

Read 2 Timothy 2:2. What characteristics do you notice about the way Paul invested in people?

How might your season of singleness change if you invested in people as Paul did?

friends

Not only was Paul surrounded by protégés, but he also had good friends. In addition to the people we're investing our lives in, we need others who can share our burdens and struggles—brothers and sisters to lock arms with. During singleness we should cultivate deep friendships. Even at the end of his life, Paul had Luke by his side. Many of us have acquaintances and coworkers we see and interact with. But here we're talking about deeper relationships that go beyond a surface level. We're talking about friends who push us forward in God's call on our lives. There's a great possibility that because Luke was a doctor, he worked to literally keep Paul's battered body alive![1]

Read King Solomon's words in Ecclesiastes 4:10. What's pitiable about someone who has no friendships?

How can you cultivate the kinds of friendships that preserve your life spiritually and physically?

a lifelong learner

Read 2 Timothy 4:13.

This is another verse that's easy to pass over, one that at first glance has nothing to do with the season of singleness. Yet Paul teaches us something valuable here.

session one 15

Even from his prison cell, even after all he had preached, all of the ministry he had done, and all he had accomplished, he wasn't finished learning.

Singleness gives you a freedom from distraction like no other time in your life. You have the time to learn and grow in a way you may not later.

Take a moment to look at your calendar. What free time do you have this month that could be directed toward learning?

What are a few ways you can build your faith during this time?

If learning doesn't come naturally to you, consider marking this priority on your calendar, blocking time each day or week to pursue learning so that like the apostle Paul, you'll continually grow in Christ.

forgiveness

Read 2 Timothy 4:14-15. Based on these verses, how would you describe Alexander?

What did Alexander oppose about Paul?

This wasn't a personality conflict. It was opposition to Paul's teaching. Any follower of Jesus should face the same challenge. Jesus warned us in Luke 6:26 that we should be wary when everyone speaks well of us. The goal isn't to proactively make enemies. But when we're taking a stand for the truth, we'll face resistance.

Paul handled Alexander's hatred with incredible maturity. Notice his reaction in verse 14. Paul didn't try to even the score or call down curses on Alexander. Just a few sentences later Paul would even forgive his friends (see verse 16). During Paul's court hearing in Rome over his imprisonment, it would have been common for supporters to come forward to vouch for Paul; defend his character; or, at the very least, plead for mercy on his behalf. Paul asked that everyone reading this letter refuse to hold a grudge against the people who had deserted him.

Based on Paul's example, what should we say and do to truly forgive someone who has wronged us?

Is forgiveness a regular practice in your life? How can you grow in the ability to forgive?

rest

It may have appeared that Paul stood alone while he was on trial, and verse 16 would lead us to believe that. Yet he wasn't alone.

Read 2 Timothy 4:17.

session one   17

God's presence filled Paul with courage to proclaim the gospel, even while on trial for proclaiming that same gospel. Paul leveraged his time in prison and his life of singleness to advance the gospel. He didn't seek to be put into prison, but he used his imprisonment as a platform for evangelism.

God can use your current circumstances as a single person as well. It's no accident that you're where you are, have the time you have, and are surrounded by the people who are a part of your life.

What about Paul's courage inspires you most?

Read Paul's closing affirmation in 2 Timothy 4:18.

Whereas most people would have ended the letter by asking for help in getting out of prison, Paul found a way to rest in God. He had a broader view of the work of God, trusting Him with his ultimate redemption and rescue. Therefore, nothing could touch him. It's impossible to control everything in life, but it's possible to be both known and loved by the Creator of life itself. This truth gave Paul peace, and it can give us peace as well.

When have you seen someone act calm in a stressful situation?

How can you apply Paul's affirmation in verse 18 to your current season in life?

When you rest in God, you recognize that your life is about your relationship with Him. The way you relate to God is far more important than the way you relate to other human beings. Identity isn't found in your friends, your dating relationships, or even your spouse. Identity is found in your relationship with Christ. He's the only person who's able to define you. When we're you in Christ, you're adopted into the family of God as a son or a daughter of the King. Ultimately, flourishing in singleness (and in every other stage) depends upon having an identity that isn't found in your relationships (or lack thereof) but in Christ.

What happens when we seek our identity in relationship with other people instead of with Christ?

When have you fallen into this trap? What were the results?

personal application

We've explored some of the ways Paul maximized his singleness. Now let's evaluate our own lives and determine how we can implement some of his practices.It's one thing to know what obedience looks like, but it's another thing to walk in the steps the Lord has directed for us.

your devotion

Read Matthew 28:19-20.

The point of life, no matter what season you're in, is to know Jesus and make Him known. Even if you feel that you're early in your journey of knowing God, you can still find ways to help others along the way. As we saw in the first portion of this session's personal study, Paul devoted his life to proclaiming the gospel and to training others to proclaim the gospel.

Based on your past experiences and current passions and reality, how can you join God on mission in this season of singleness?

Who are some people in your city, community, or church you believe you could help?

How could you help those people on their journeys of knowing Jesus more and making Him known?

An old African proverb says, "If you do not initiate the boys, they will burn the village down." Paul charged Timothy to entrust the truths of God to reliable people who can teach others (see 2 Timothy 2:2). This is often called the four-generation verse:

PAUL ➤ TIMOTHY ➤ RELIABLE PEOPLE ➤ OTHERS

Are there people in your life who follow this process well? What are some of the things they do?

Do you have a mentor in your life who's helping you know Jesus better? If not, how could you position yourself to get one?

What would it look like for you to invest your time and energy in helping others know Jesus?

your friends

Even in his final hours Paul had a close friend beside him. In our season of singleness, we need deep friendships—the kind who can stand the test of time and endure difficulties, people who know us, love us, and hold us accountable for stewarding the ministry and relationships God has entrusted to us. These friendships aren't easy to come by, but they're worth the effort to find and nurture.

Whom have you given permission to speak truth into your life? What are their names?

Do you truly trust these people in the deepest recesses of your heart? When was the last time you actively demonstrated that you trust them at that level? How did they respond?

If you don't have that kind of friendship, what steps could you take in this season to begin developing one?

a lifelong learner

In 2 Timothy 4:13 we looked at Paul's example of being a lifelong learner. Even in His last days Paul was committed to knowing God better. Singleness provides a unique opportunity to invest deeply in our relationship with God.

What's your plan to learn and grow in this season?

Try this activity this week. Spend thirty minutes a day reading, in addition to the time you spend reading the Scriptures. Select a book or a Bible study that will help you grow spiritually. If you're not sure where to start, consult a pastor or a godly friend. Then commit to read for thirty minutes. If you do this every day, in addition to growing spiritually, the University of Michigan's annual health-and-retirement study says you'll live an average of two additional years.[2]

Record your progress.

DAY 1: I read _____ minutes. I read _____ pages.

DAY 2: I read _____ minutes. I read _____ pages.

DAY 3: I read _____ minutes. I read _____ pages.

DAY 4: I read _____ minutes. I read _____ pages.

DAY 5: I read _____ minutes. I read _____ pages.

DAY 6: I read _____ minutes. I read _____ pages.

DAY 7: I read _____ minutes. I read _____ pages.

What was difficult about this activity?

What was rewarding?

How can you ensure that learning is an ongoing part of your life?

forgiving people from your past

This may be one of your most important pursuits as a single person. Like everyone else, you've been hurt, and hurt people eventually hurt other people. Forgiveness isn't minimizing the wrongs or the pain. Instead, it's choosing to maximize your view of God even in the midst of pain and confusion and allowing God to enforce justice as only He can. In Romans 12:19 Paul reminds us that vengeance and repayment for wrongs belong to the Lord Himself.

Make a list of the people who've hurt you in the past.

Read 1 Peter 2:20-23.

We must learn to forgive as Jesus did. He took the wrongs committed against Him and "entrusted himself to the one who judges justly" (verse 23).

Describe what forgiveness would look like if you granted it to the people who've hurt you the most.

Beginning to verbalize your forgiveness can prepare you for the day when you'll have the opportunity to offer those people the same kind of forgiveness Jesus offered you. If you have difficulty forgiving, consult a counselor. At the very least, call a trusted friend and walk through this process with him or her.

People on mission need to be forgiving people. As we've seen, opposition can accompany living on mission. Paul was a man on a mission, and he encountered opposition. This wasn't just a generic "Life was tough for Paul." This resistance had a name: Alexander (see 2 Timothy 4:14-15). Note that their contention wasn't a personality conflict. It was Alexander's opposition to Paul's message. Paul was so closely associated with Jesus that if someone hated Jesus, they hated Paul. We're meant to be this way. We don't need to be needlessly offensive, but throughout the Scriptures we're told that those who live a godly life will be persecuted.

When we stand for the truth, our lives themselves become offensive, as Paul's was. Have you ever faced opposition because of your association with Jesus? What happened?

Paul was willing to go to jail for his association with Jesus. Has your faith ever cost you anything? If not, why not?

Paul was thrown into prison for his faith. It's hard to think when Paul started his journey with Jesus, he would proclaim the truth while bound in chains. The reality is that living in a fallen world means not everybody will receive our faith with open arms.

rest

Writing from prison, Paul was in the most stressful place imaginable, where his life was on the line and he could die any day. Yet he was at rest.

Read 2 Corinthians 4:16-17.

Paul reminds us that the pain, setbacks, and frustrations of life are only momentary in the grand scope of eternity. And even though we're wasting away on the outside, daily spiritual renewal occurs internally.

What stresses you out most?

What does it look like for you to trust in God and His plans even in the middle of your stress?

How are you being internally renewed every day?

NOTES

1. 1. This idea is adapted from Tommy Nelson, the pastor of Denton Bible Church.

2. "Health and Retirement Study," accessed January 23, 2019, http://hrsonline.isr.umich.edu/.

journal

If seeking God through prayer and Scripture reading is difficult for you because you can't seem to find the time, try blocking off fifteen minutes each day over the next week to meet with God.

Create calendar events each day of the next week for activities like the following.

• Stop what you're doing and pray.

• Read three chapters in the Bible.

• Read three verses of Scripture over and over again.

• Memorize one Bible verse.

Use the chart on the next page to outline Scriptures you'll read and where and when you'll read them. Afterward list one prayer and one truth you learned.

At the end of the week, evaluate whether fifteen minutes were enough. Would you like to block off more time next week?

	scripture	time & place	prayer	truth
sunday				
monday				
tuesday				
wednesday				
thursday				
friday				
saturday				

session two

who to date

group study

start

Welcome to session two.

① High + low of your day

Last week we focused on the season of singleness. This season isn't just a quick stop on the way to something greater. Rather, it's a phase unlike any other in our lives, when our undistracted devotion gives us an opportunity to root our primary identity in Christ.

② Did anything stick out to you?

If you fully applied all you learned from the Scriptures about singleness last week, how would you be shaped into the man or the woman God has created to share life with someone else?

→ You attract what you are.

Though the goal of singleness isn't to rush through the phase, most of us eventually move to the next season of dating. The word itself conjures up a range of thoughts and emotions for most of us, from confusion to euphoria, from joy and happiness to drama and disappointment. Most of us don't approach this topic with a blank slate but with years of accumulated thoughts and experiences. [Every day we're inundated with images and stories of dating by our friends and social-media feeds, leaving us with loads of bias.]

K: **Are you currently in the season of dating? How long have you been in it? What's your funniest dating story?**

K: **What qualities do you look for when deciding whether to date someone?**

The focus this week isn't about getting a date. Anybody can get a date if they lower their standards enough. The goal is to date the right person in the right way. If you've ever dated someone, you know how difficult this goal can be. The challenge of this season has caused some of us to grow cynical, either completely giving up on dating or giving up on finding God's best. Although the Bible doesn't say anything about dating, it says plenty about how we're to evaluate someone as we pursue a relationship. This process of dating begins with the question, *Who should I date?*

this session's topic

Use this section to provide necessary context for the session's topic.

Men and women are choosing to get married later and later in life. Though many factors contribute to this trend, one major contributor to our confusion is the lack of clarity about what exactly we should be looking for! If the process of dating exists to evaluate another person, then what criteria should we use to evaluate them? What constitutes a good fit for a husband or a wife? We've rarely, if ever, slowed down long enough to evaluate whether our expectations in relatioships are realistic and whether they line up with God's design.

The answer to the question, Who should I date? revolves around two words: *character* and *chemistry*. We're looking for a person who has *character* before God and *chemistry* with us. Who we date sets the stage for every phase of life that follows. This week we'll chart a course that will help us determine the type of person who's worth pursuing as a lifelong partner.

Pray together; then begin video session two.

watch

Use these statements to follow along as you watch video session two.

You are made for community.

*He gave the apostles, the prophets, the evangelists, the shepherds
and teachers, to equip the saints for the work of ministry,
for building up the body of Christ, until we all attain to the unity
of the faith and of the knowledge of the Son of God, to mature manhood,
to the measure of the stature of the fullness of Christ.*
EPHESIANS 4:11-13

Communities form around causes.

Our communion is around the eternal Son of God.

What Kind of Person Should You Date?

1. Someone with the same cause

2. Someone with character

3. Someone with whom you have chemistry

Use these questions to discuss the video teaching.

What words would you use to describe your experiences dating?

Ben opened with a story about a time when he and his friends climbed Long's Peak, the tallest mountain in the Rockies. As they climbed higher and higher, they began to run out of energy. An older guy stopped, taught them how to breathe in their new environment, and encouraged them to keep going.

How have you seen the environment of dating change since you began this journey? What are some new rules of engagement and expectations that have been placed on this season?

Ben said, "A higher level of connectivity has given us less community." How has our culture's rapid adoption of smartphones and technology affected your personal sense of community?

Genesis 2:18 records, "The Lord God said, 'It is not good for the man to be alone. I will make a helper corresponding to him.'" Most of us read that verse only through the lens of a marriage relationship. The broader principle is that God created us for deep, authentic relationships. "It's just me and God" isn't enough. We were made for community.

Who's your community right now? Is it composed of people who are driving you toward Jesus? How do you know?

Read aloud Ephesians 4:11-16. What does this passage say about our uniqueness?

Do you feel that your community "promotes the growth of the body for building up itself in love by the proper working of each individual part" (verse 16)? In what ways?

Communities often unite around causes and interests. The extent to which that cause endures often marks the extent to which the community relationships endure. Eternal causes lead to eternal communities.

> **How have changing circumstances changed your community? What cause is your community built on right now?**

The person we should date often comes from the same community we're working to create and be a part of. Ben encouraged us to remember three primary guidelines as we decide who we should date:

1. FIND SOMEONE WHO HAS THE SAME CAUSE AS YOU.

2. FIND SOMEONE WHO HAS YOUR SAME CHARACTER, SHAPED BY GOD.

3. FIND SOMEONE WITH WHOM YOU SHARE CHEMISTRY.

> **Recall a previous dating relationship. Which of these did your date fail to fulfill? Which did you fail to fulfill for your date?**

In Genesis 24 Abraham sent his servant to find a wife for his son, Isaac. His first charge was "Don't find a wife among the Canaanites!" (see verse 3). Why? Because the people of Canaan didn't pursue the Lord, nor did they have character that had been chiseled by Him. Abraham's servant had to walk five hundred miles to find the right person for Isaac.

> **Is your current community filled with people who have a cause and character worth pursuing? If not, what needs to change?**

pray

* Read to page 112

Close the session with prayer.

Kelsey:

Ask God to help the group be concerned with *being* the right type of person before *finding* the right person. Pray that you won't be so focused on figuring out who to date that you don't develop your own character and relationship with Him.

personal study

abraham // biblical case study

The longest chapter in Genesis is about finding a wife. This is good news for us for two reasons.

1. It shows us that God cares about our dating life and our desire to be married.

2. The narrative in that chapter provides us with principles that will help us evaluate a potential mate.

Starting in Genesis 12, the author, Moses, began to focus on a single family, the family of Abraham. God had made a promise to Abraham that all the nations of the world would be blessed through his offspring, but as Abraham's life neared its end, one outstanding challenge remained: finding a wife for his son, Isaac. Without a wife the family line couldn't continue. The approach Abraham took looks a bit different from ours today, but the narrative contains principles that can be applied to our modern context.

a serious commitment

Read Genesis 24:2.

When planning to find a wife for his son (arranged marriages were the practice in that day), Abraham called his most trusted servant and made him swear in the Lord's name with one of the most serious of oaths in that day. Why this ceremony? Because Abraham knew that the person Isaac married would have more influence on him than any other person. Therefore, a wise person approaches the process of finding a spouse with an appropriate amount of seriousness.

In today's world we don't take the question of who we should date quite so seriously. Our casual approach to dating doesn't always reflect the seriousness with which God takes marriage.

How could you apply Abraham's covenant in deciding who you should date?

Who do you feel close enough to ask for help in becoming more intentional and focused about deciding who to date?

One reason our dating relationships are so stressful is that we don't have a goal in mind. How is dating reframed when marriage is the goal?

Abraham was serious because marriage is serious. As we've seen and will continue to see, dating exists for evaluation. Dating provides spaces and context to evaluate whether you should marry someone. This doesn't mean you should on every date expecting to marry the person sitting across from you. However, it does mean you should discontinue the relationship at the point it becomes clear that marriage isn't an option. To do that, you need to be armed with the proper criterion for evaluation.

the right criterion

Read Genesis 24:3-4.

Abraham was commanding his servant to find a wife for his son who was of the same faith. Abraham wasn't advocating for racism in dating, though at first glance it may appear so. He told his servant not to get a Canaanite woman, because these people were polytheists, with the worship of their gods centering on violence. These beliefs and practices stood at odds with Abraham's primary criterion for dating. In fact, the only criterion Abraham specified was that the woman must be a believer in the one true God. And he was sending his servant on a journey of over five hundred miles to find her!

Maybe the person God has for you isn't part of your current relational circle, just as Isaac's future wife wasn't part of his.

How does Abraham's servant's journey of over five hundred miles to find Mrs. Right give you courage on your journey?

What adjustments might you need to make in order to better position yourself to meet a potential mate?

Read Genesis 24:5-7. Does this request seem to be too demanding for Abraham to make of his future daughter-in-law? Why or why not?

In one of the most significant moments in all of Scripture, God had called Abraham to move to a specific place with his family (see 12:1-3). As the story of Scripture unfolds, we discover why: God wanted Abraham's distant descendant, Jesus, to be born, live, die, and rise from the dead on the one piece of land that unites three major continents. So Abraham's family had moved by faith. For Isaac to leave and go back to the old country would be to walk away from God's clear call. In our modern circumstances this would be the equivalent of a potential mate encouraging us to violate God's expressed will for our lives found in the Scriptures. We just can't do it.

who to date

What godly qualities did you notice in the woman Abraham was looking for in these verses? What other qualities reflect a godly heart that you'd add to the list?

don't compromise

Read Genesis 24:8.

Notice the resolve in Abraham's instruction. If the servant didn't find the right woman, he was free to come home. If seeking marriage and living for God found themselves at odds, Abraham said, "Choose God!"

In deciding who we'll date, compromise is only one decision away. And with every compromising step we take, our hearts become more and more calloused. Abraham wasn't willing to give an inch. Neither should we. More often than not, we feel that compromise happens after we begin dating someone, when we're tempted to compromise our standards of sexual and emotional purity. But integrity starts well before that.

In Ephesians 4 Paul cautioned the Ephesians about a number of different sins. Then he said, "Don't give the devil an opportunity" (verse 27) Other Bible versions translate *opportunity* as "foothold" (NIV, NLT).

Read Ephesians 4:25-27. What did Paul mean by using the word *opportunity*? Why might the devil want an opportunity with the person we date?

Why are we often willing to ignore red flags in our dating relationships?

Opportunity in verse 27 means "a place to exert influence." Opportunity happens often in dating relationships. That's why we need to focus on the quality and character of the people we date.

Genesis 24:14 gives us an even clearer picture of who we should date. In fact, we see two primary character qualities.

character and chemistry

Read Genesis 24:10-21.

God won't always reveal His choice like this. It would be nice if we could pray, "Lord, let the person I sit beside at the coffee shop today be my future spouse," and they show up. However, it's significant to see the types of activities this servant hoped to find the woman engaged in.

Abraham's servant was hoping the woman would offer to give water to his camels, so he was looking for someone who was gracious and hospitable, even to a stranger. The implications are huge for relationships today. Our posture toward hospitality and generosity speaks volumes about our character and love for people. These were qualities Abraham was looking for in a wife for his son.

Why do you think graciousness was so important to Abraham? By implication, why should it be important to us?

Read Genesis 24:56-59. Record some qualities of Rebekah's faith that you see in this passage.

Usually when we talk about having chemistry with someone, we're talking about physical compatibility. Although this is important, it's not the only form of chemistry we should look for. Through observation Rebekah realized she had chemistry with Isaac. She observed his faith and theological compatibility (see verses 26-27), his vocational compatibility (Abraham's servant had brought camels with him, verse. 10), and his social compatibility (Abraham's servant stayed with her family, verse 31). These factors of chemistry and compatibility are vital in deciding who we'll date.

Toward which facets of chemistry do you first gravitate?

On which quality are you tempted to compromise—character or chemistry? Explain.

Both character and chemistry should drive us in deciding who to date. When we focus on only one quality, we'll ultimately be disappointed. But when we prioritize both characteristics, we're likely to find people worth dating.

personal application

In this section we're going to get more personal. Instead of simply looking at what Scripture says, we're going to explore how we can live by the truth.

personal faith

Read Hebrews 11:6-20.

Hebrews 11 provides some commentary on what we learned about Abraham and Isaac in Genesis 24. The short story: they were men who lived by faith. They believed God rewards those who seek Him, and their belief influenced their actions. In Genesis 24 Rebecca proved to be a great match for Isaac because she lived by faith as well. Her confidence in God gave her boldness to walk across the desert, as well as kindness to care for the camels of the aging servant. For both Isaac and Rebecca, their active faith was their most attractive trait.

In this week's study you've likely been focusing on who you should date, an incredibly important decision. But if the person you should date also read this lesson, would they choose you because of your faith? In other words, are you someone they should date?

Does your faith in God influence your actions? In what ways?

Rebecca's faith manifested itself in bold confidence in God and gentleness with others. Do you see those characteristics in your life? Why or why not?

What changes do you need to make that could shape your life into the kind of person Abraham was looking for on behalf of his son?

who to date

character

Read 1 Peter 3:3-4.

Peter wasn't saying you should never dress up. He was saying your character will take you further than your cosmetics. This is true whether you're a guy or a girl.

Have you ever valued your physical appearance more than your character? If so, how?

In what ways have you used your physical beauty to try to manipulate God's timing and plans for you?

Often we know what we value by the way we spend our time and money. If you look at someone's budget and calendar, you'll clearly see what's most important to them. You can say you treasure something, but if you never spend time and energy and resources pursuing it, your words don't match your actions.

If someone looked only at your budget and calendar, what would they say is most valuable to you?

Abraham had sealed his intentions with a covenant—a powerful symbolic gesture signifying his intent to pursue God at any cost. His confidence in God's guidance (see Genesis 24:7) fueled his commitment to God's standards. He was willing for his servant to walk away from any woman who wasn't God's best.

Do you believe God will take care of you, even in your dating life? If not, why?

In what ways are you tempted to settle for something less than God's best?

In Genesis 24 we read that Abraham's pursuit of a wife for Isaac was marked by graciousness and kindness. Let's look at some implications those qualities have for our lives.

for women

Read Proverbs 11:16.

A woman isn't gracious so that others will notice. You've no doubt seen that kind of self-serving generosity. But at the same time, her generosity doesn't go unnoticed. That's what the word *honor* implies. Others notice and give her honor.

Have you ever put graciousness and honor together? Why might the Bible link them like this?

How do you know that someone is gracious? Describe them.

who to date

Would other people say you're a gracious person?

Ask a guy friend whether he finds graciousness and generosity attractive in a woman. Why or why not? Record his response.

for men

Proverbs 19:22 says, "What is desirable in a man is his kindness" (NASB). That's pretty clear! Men, if you want to be desirable, choose kindness. To be kind means to be friendly, generous, and considerate of others.

What have you done this month that's kind to others?

If your friends were honest, would they say you're known for kindness? If not, why is this a trait worth developing?

Ask a woman whether she finds kindness in a man attractive. Why or why not? Record her response.

don't compromise

In deciding who we'll date, compromise is only one decision away. And with every compromising step we take, our hearts become more and more calloused.

In what ways have you compromised in the past when choosing someone to date?

What ramifications did compromising have for your spiritual life?

Are you compromising now? If so, what steps need to be taken to stop?

Read Hebrews 3:12-13.

Rarely does compromise in huge areas of your life happen out of the blue. You don't go from a devout follower of Jesus to a hardened criminal with one decision as you're driving down the road one evening. Following Jesus in every area of your life is a daily decision you must make, and seemingly minor departures from that commitment take you on a path that can have disastrous consequences over time.

That's why verse 13 says you need encouragement daily. Not just weekly or monthly or yearly. You need it every day. If you don't receive it, you're in danger of being hardened by sin's deceitfulness. This prospect ought to sober you. When you're deciding who you'll date, Satan would love to deceive you and lull you into compromising in small, unseen, "This won't hurt anyone" areas of your life that begin to callous your heart. Encouragement by other believers fights against compromise. You must have other people in your life who know you, care for you, and speak truth to you. If you want to turn away "from the living God" (verse 12), find some friends who will encourage you to pursue Jesus with every ounce of your being.

Who do you trust enough to honestly share your struggles and failings with?

Why do we all need this person? If you don't currently have a go-to person, who could you ask to fill this gap?

Is this person encouraging you to fight against the deception of sin?

Your pursuit of who to date is vitally important to your spiritual life. Don't make this decision by yourself and risk starting your dating season with the wrong person. The human heart is too easily led astray to be fully trusted. Find some encouragers who will help you see with sober eyes and begin to pursue the right person without compromise.

journal

As you've studied Genesis 24 this week, you've seen that Abraham's standards matched Rebekah's character. Let's look at the qualities that told Abraham's servant that Rebekah was the right woman for Isaac.

What are some nonnegotiable qualities of the person you would agree to date? Identify qualities without which you would refuse to date that person, even when you're feeling weak and ready to compromise.

If you're not currently dating someone and would like to, record a prayer asking God to give you wisdom to recognize the right person to date.

If you're currently dating someone, record a prayer thanking God for the person you're with. Ask Him to give you wisdom to recognize whether their character reflects the heart of God.

session three

how to date

group study

Welcome to session three.

We've discovered that singleness exists so that we can live with undistracted devotion to the Lord. This goal is best pursued with a community that's pursuing Him with equal passion. Within that community, by the grace of God, you might meet someone you believe has a God-shaped character and a fun, easy chemistry with you. Now comes the big question. What do you do? How do you move from "What's your name?" to "Until death do us part"? Throughout history this process has looked different. In much of the world today, we engage in a process known as dating. But it might be truly said today that this process is more confusing than ever. The ambiguity in modern dating can produce much anxiety.

How would you describe the modern dating scene? What are the upsides? What are the downsides?

Would you say you've enjoyed dating? Has the way you've approached dating led you to the types of people we talked about in the previous section? Why or why not?

Dating has the potential to be frightening or fun, encouraging or depressing.
→ While ambiguity in modern dating can produce anxiety, some clarity about the process can bring much-needed comfort. The good news is that the same God who cares about who you marry also cares about how you get to know them.

Question:
Describe the ideal first date.

What's your most memorable date? Why?

"making it work" vs. "is my life better with them?"

this session's topic

Use this section to provide necessary context for the session's topic.

The Bible doesn't talk about dating per se. No verses tell you where to take your date out to eat or what movie theater to go to. No Scripture references tell you how long a date should last, what you should say, whether you should text after your date, or how long the dating season should last. In fact, dating, as our culture currently defines it, isn't a biblical concept.

Nevertheless, the Bible provides principles that help us properly evaluate whether someone is the right fit as a marriage partner. That's what dating truly is: an evaluation. As we approach this crucial topic from a biblical standpoint, we want to design dating to reveal whether the person we're with is the right one for us. After all, we may spend the rest of our lives with this person. Dating is a process, meaning it's characterized by movement. It's not an end in itself but has a predetermined destination: marriage.

This week we'll explore biblical principles that help guide us through dating. These don't provide a step-by-step guide to be followed. Relating to people is much more complex and dynamic than following a recipe for baking a chocolate cake. However, the good news is that if you follow these guiding principles and apply them to the dynamic environment of dating, they'll help you on your journey and give you confidence to honor God in your dating decisions.

Pray together; then begin video session three.

watch

Use these statements to follow along as you watch video session three.

Dating is the process of evaluating whether or not we're supposed to run along with somebody for a lifetime.

How We Evaluate

1. We date with clarity.

2. We date with autonomy.

3. We date with purity.

 Dating is a process of evaluation. It is not a status to sit in.

Sex subverts the evaluation process.

Get surrounded by good community.

7 principles of dating:
① Prayer
↳ Trust God with your life

discuss

Use these questions to discuss the video teaching.

Maybe you're at a place in your life where you've decided you'd like to share it with another person. That's a good, God-given desire. It was God who said, "It is not good for the man to be alone" (Genesis 2:18). Knowing that desiring a mate is a good one, the question we have to answer is, How do we find the right person?

> **In his talk Ben defined *dating* as the process of evaluating whether we're supposed to run along with somebody for a lifetime. How is it helpful to think of dating as a process of evaluation?**

Although it's true that dating isn't a biblical practice, evaluation is. Ben pointed out that marriage doesn't magically change someone. Seeing dating as a time to evaluate helps us understand and find what we're looking for in a mate.

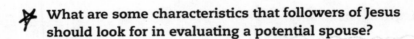 **What are some characteristics that followers of Jesus should look for in evaluating a potential spouse?**

> **In what ways are these characteristics different from the broader cultural ideas of how to find a mate?**

Ben challenged us to date with clarity, speaking the truth in love (see Ephesians 4:15). We don't play games with another person. As we initiate with clarity, seek clarity in the process, and offer clarity when we have it, we honor the other person.

> **Ben called clarity a gift we can give each other. Why is clarity so helpful in the dating process?**

> **What can you say or ask to offer clarity from the very beginning of a dating relationship?**

how to date

At every stage of the dating process, we should seek to honor the person we're dating by giving them clarity, both about what we want and about how we feel. Clarity comes from confidence, which we build in two ways.

This is Good!!

1. PRACTICE. The more you practice giving clarity, the more confidence you'll possess.

2. TRUSTING GOD. God is looking out for you no matter how this relationship goes.

> **How do you build your confidence more—in practice or in trusting God? Explain.**

Another frequent question that comes up in our dating lives is, What are the obligations of dating? We need to remember that dating is a process to move through, not a status to sit in. Therefore, we need to date with autonomy. Much of the confusion we find in dating comes from a misunderstanding of what dating is.

> **Read 1 Timothy 5:1b-2. How are we supposed to treat the people we date? What are some rules or practices we've placed on dating that are more cultural than biblical?**

> **How does our community help us in the process of evaluation? What are some ways we can seek to intentionally involve people who are close to us in our dating process?**

prayer

Close the session with prayer.

Ask God to help the group gain clarity through this season of dating. Pray for clarity to know and for courage to act on His best plan for you. Confess your desire to honor God individually and collectively through your dating lives.

personal study

abraham's servant // biblical case study

Last week we looked at an Old Testament story in which Abraham sent out his top aide to find a wife for Isaac, Abraham's son. This account showed us that the right person is worth pursuing and waiting for. This same biblical story also provides principles for dating in a way that honors God

start in the right place

Read Genesis 24:9-10.

If you're going to date the right person in the right way, you've got to start by going to the right place. Nahor was Abraham's brother, and Abraham sent his servant to Nahor's town to search for a wife for Isaac. This makes sense, right? Abraham was looking for someone from his family, so he sent his servant to the town where his family lived. There weren't many believers in God in Canaan, but more could be found among his relatives in the old country. So when it was time to choose a wife for Isaac, he sent his servant to the area with the highest concentration of believers. Yet today we don't often make that explicit connection. If we're looking for a man after God's heart, we should go to places where men after God's heart congregate. If we want a woman who prizes godly character, it follows that we should search for them in places where they might be found.

Have the places you've been looking put you into contact with people who share your faith? If not, why do you keep looking there?

Where are some places you might find a higher percentage of potential dates who follow Jesus?

As we continue to read, notice that Abraham's servant didn't just arrive in the right town; his pursuit was more specific than that.

Read Genesis 24:11. What do you notice about the kind of women who would be out at this time of day? Why is this detail significant?

Throughout the Bible godly women were those who were willing to work hard. A woman who's willing to work is a prize. On the contrary, a lazy person will frustrate you to no end. To date the right person in the right way, you've got to look for someone who puts their gifts into action.

start with the right posture

In addition to beginning in the right place, we must date with the right posture.

Read Genesis 24:12-14.

Abraham's servant humbly asked God for success in finding the right person. Notice at the beginning and the end of the prayer he invoked God's "steadfast love," "lovingkindness," or "kindness." These various words all translate the Hebrew word *hesed,* which refers to God's loyal love, a major theme in the Old Testament. This love binds God to His people, promising not to let go. The servant rooted the search for a spouse in his understanding that God cherished and promised to be with His people. He was confident that God cared about this search because He knew God cared about His people.

Have you ever prayed a similar prayer? Why or why not?

Do you believe God cares about your dating life? How would it change the way you perceive relationships if you knew God was invested in the search with you?

strive for clarity

So you think you might have found someone worth dating. Congrats! What now? What should you do when you meet someone you think you'd like to know better?

INITIATE THE DATING RELATIONSHIP WITH CLARITY. Truthfully express your thoughts and intentions. Much of the anguish in modern dating could be alleviated if we mustered the courage to graciously tell each other what we think, how we feel, and what we'd like to do. Though it might feel easier in the moment to travel the path of ambiguity, establishing clarity serves both parties well. We can give each other the gift of freedom from anxiety simply by providing clarity.

Read Ephesians 4:15. What does this truth have to do with dating and clarity?

Have you ever failed to provide clarity in a dating relationship? How did the lack of clarity make the other person feel?

how to date

When have you seen clarity (truth) expressed in dating? What was the result?

Abraham's servant gave clarity as soon as he knew this meeting was from the Lord, placing a ring in Rebekah's nose and bracelets on her arm (see Genesis 24:22, NIV). These gifts conveyed a lot of symbolism, and Rebekah, along with all who witnessed this event, would have readily understood their significance. These gifts demonstrated a clear intention—marriage. Although you may not give someone a nose ring and bracelets on your first date, Abraham's servant made his intentions clear, and so should we. You may not know whether you intend to marry this person after the first date, but you can still offer clarity about what you know. Being vague or obtuse doesn't help anyone.

Simple statements like "I'd like to get to know you. Could we go to dinner sometime?" help clarify relationships from the beginning. At the end of a date, asking, "Can I call you?" sets a clear expectation. If things aren't working out, saying so gracefully lets the other person off the hook. No one likes being left in limbo. Dating with clarity eliminates heartache and frustration.

What does clarity look like in a dating relationship?

How can you begin offering appropriate clarity from the very first date?

Read Genesis 24:54-59. What question was asked in this passage? Who asked it?

Even your friends and family want clarity about your dating relationships. You give them peace when you offer clarity by sharing what's going on. You don't have to be fully open with everyone you encounter. That wouldn't be wise. However, clarity reaches beyond just you and your dating partner. Giving clarity to your community allows them to speak into your dating process for the better. The more clarity you can offer those closest to you, the more they'll be at peace, and the better they can guide you to discover whether this is the right person for you.

WATCH AND LEARN. Clarity is an ever-growing process, aided by time and observation. Because dating is primarily designed to allow you to determine whether the other person is the right fit, you should prioritize that period of your life. That priority is reflected in Genesis 24.

Read Genesis 24:21. What kinds of activities do you think the servant observed Rebekah doing?

How do you think he measured success?

It's one thing to hear what someone says. It's entirely different to watch the way they live. It's one thing to delve into someone's social-media account. It's another thing to watch them in live action.

Read Proverbs 31:30. Why is charm so deceptive?

What are you inclined to believe when you're with someone who's charming?

Anybody can be charming for an hour on a first date. There's nothing wrong with charm, but it doesn't tell the whole story. We need time to learn whether character lies beneath it. We should watch; observe; and learn in multiple, varied environments.

By starting in the right spot, praying honestly, seeking and offering clarity, and observing the other person in action, you can begin to date with wisdom and intentionality.

Based on today's study, what's one thing you'll do differently on future dates?

In the previous section we explored the *how* of dating from a biblical standpoint. We highlighted starting in the right place, praying, striving for clarity, and watching to learn. Let's look at these actions more closely and apply them to our hearts. Not only do we want to know what the Bible says, but we also want to ask ourselves, *Does the way I date reflect these biblical truths?*

start in the right place

It's hard to imagine dating well if you don't start well. It's like trying to start a road trip with a car that needs repairs. You might make it part of the way down the road, but you'll be forced to pull over soon when your car breaks down. Abraham sent his servant to look among his own people, believers in the one true God, not among the Canaanites (see Genesis 24:1-4).

Have you committed to God that you won't choose a spouse from "the Canaanites," people who don't serve the one true God? Why should you?

What do we miss in our relationships if we're not aligned in our faith?

Where do you currently look for dates? Do these locations include an abundance of people who are seeking God's heart?

List some places where people who place the same priority
on a relationship with God tend to gather.

pray, trusting for provision

When Jesus taught us to pray in Matthew 6, He said, "Give us today our daily
bread" (verses 10-11). He could have taught us to say, "God, bless us today" or
"God, help me." God knows what we need each day. Asking Him for daily bread
should lead us to trust His provision.

Our prayers about dating should reflect this truth.

**How can your prayers for a mate help you learn to trust God
and His provision for you?**

provide clarity

Proverbs 24:26 says an honest answer is "a kiss on the lips." Honesty doesn't
mean a full disclosure of every thought in your head. But conversely, ambiguity
is the seedbed of anxiety. A lack of clarity in a dating relationship can
produce anxiety.

**Why do you think Proverbs 24:26 describes an honest answer
as "a kiss on the lips"?**

**Has your own lack of clarity in dating made others feel
uncertain or anxious? If so, how or why?**

What do you need to do to provide more clarity in your current relationship? How can you get it?

Clarity is needed at the initiation stage, throughout the dating process, and at the end if a relationship needs to end. Honesty needs to prevail in each of those instances. First Corinthians 14:33 tells us that God is a God of peace, not confusion. Therefore, each time you leave someone with confusion, you fail to reflect the character of God. But each time you lead with clarity and conviction, even in painful moments when relationships die, you shine with the character of God.

What does it look like to exit a relationship with clarity and honesty?

Have you ever seen a relationship that ended well, leaving peace without confusion?

Much of the angst in dating stems from viewing dating as a status to sit in rather than a process to move through. In our culture we find a desire to create a separate, interim category called "We're dating," marked by boyfriend and girlfriend status. As we try to enter this sphere, the question immediately rises, What are the rules now that we're boyfriend and girlfriend? For example:

• Was he supposed to text me immediately after that date?

• Was she supposed to let me know she's not available?

• Shouldn't he have checked with me first?

• Is it OK if we _____?

• How far is too far?

how to date

You've probably asked most of these questions yourself. You may have even searched the Scriptures trying to find answers. The problem is that the Bible doesn't use the categories of boyfriend and girlfriend. Biblically, you're either single or married. We maintain full autonomy until we're married.

One problem with this arrangement is that we can linger in a relationship for too long. We know it has no future but stay in it for months (or years!) because we enjoy the physical benefits, think it's better than nothing, or want to avoid the awkwardness of a breakup. But this isn't a kind way to treat each other. While we shouldn't necessarily rush into marriage, we shouldn't languish in an unclear dating status either. We should move through the process as fast as we can and as slow as we must. We can also develop the dangerous mindset that because this person is my girlfriend or boyfriend, we can relate to each other in a sexual way. But we play a dangerous game with each other's emotions when we begin to bond physically before we've committed to love a person for life.

First Timothy 5:1-2 gives us a strong guiding principle. These verses are worth printing and laminating so that you won't forget it:

> *Treat . . . older women as mothers, and younger women*
> *as sisters, with absolute purity.*
> **1 TIMOTHY 5:1-2, NIV**

Paul teaches us to treat older and younger women as mothers and sisters. If dating isn't a category the Bible recognizes, any woman who isn't your wife is either older or younger than you, so by Paul's words she's either a mother or a sister to be treated with purity.

As a single person, you have no right to the other person's body, time, or resources, and you have no claim on their life. They don't belong to you. She's a daughter of God and your sister in Jesus. He's a son of God and your brother in Jesus.

How have you used the title boyfriend or girlfriend to gain certain privileges with another person?

What does it look like to treat someone as a brother or a sister in Christ?

In what ways is that behavior different in a dating relationship, if at all?

You gain clarity when you rationally evaluate compatibility and ask people you trust to speak into the process. Answer the following questions of your current dating partner. If you aren't in a relationship, answer them as expectations for future compatibility.

Is our faith compatible? Do we both believe that Jesus is our only hope and that the purpose of life is to know Him and make Him known?

Are we socially compatible? Do we get along with each other, and do we as a couple get along with others?

Are we vocationally compatible? Do our vocational aspirations work together?

watch and learn

We saw in Genesis 24 that Abraham's servant observed Rebekah so that he could learn more about her. How do you know whether a person is reliable? You observe them in multiple environments through different situations over time. You watch the way they interact with others, the way they spend their money, the way and when they pursue Jesus, and how they use their free time.

If you're currently in a dating relationship, what actions reveal that the person is reliable?

How do they treat their friends and family? What can you learn about their reliability by observing them in the context of other relationships?

What's a reasonable length of time to determine whether someone you're dating is trustworthy and filled with integrity?

journal

Talk with a married couple you respect before the next group session. Having experienced dating, they have wisdom they can share with you. Even if they didn't perfectly execute their season of dating, you can learn from their successes and failures. Ask them the following questions and record their answers.

Where did you meet?

What qualities about your spouse were you drawn to?

How long did you date before you could confidently say your spouse was someone to whom you could entrust the rest of your life?

What kinds of dates were most helpful in evaluating whether your spouse was the right person for you?

How did you determine compatibility in the following areas?

• Faith

• Social

• Vocational

session four

pursuing purity

group study

Welcome to session four.

In this session we'll continue exploring how to date in a healthy way. We've engaged with the idea that dating is the modern process of evaluating whether we're meant to marry another person. Because it's a process of evaluation, we've asked ourselves what kind of person we should be looking for and what methods we should use to discern whether we've found them. Always before us is the end goal that we aren't looking for someone in whose eyes we can find complete fulfillment; rather, we're searching for a partner we can grip hands with and run together in pursuit of the grand purpose of knowing God and leveraging our lives for His glory.

What stood out to you most in last week's study?

What did you find challenging as you completed the personal study for session three?

What did you learn from your conversation with a married couple?

Sex is a great idea—arguably one of God's best ideas. Though he made it to be a fun experience shared by people who cherish each other deeply, all around the world we see a misuse of sexuality, causing an incredible amount of pain. Around the globe a good gift is often used in a bad way. In the midst of the chaos, the Scriptures show us a better way.

this session's topic

Use this section to provide necessary context for the session's topic.

Casual sex is becoming more and more common. The Centers for Disease Control reported that cases of chlamydia, gonorrhea, and syphilis rose to record numbers in 2017.[1] Forty-three percent of American men and 9 percent of American women report using pornography within the past week.[2] The choices we make may appear casual, but they're laced with consequences. Divorce rates dramatically increase when one spouse begins viewing pornography.[3]

Studies have also shown a significant increase in self-reported loneliness and depression in college students today, compared to previous generations. Loneliness is thought to be even more detrimental to health than smoking.[4]

So what are we to do with this season of dating? Although the Bible doesn't speak specifically about the roles of boyfriend and girlfriend, we can determine much about the way we should act toward each other through a close study of key Scriptures. God hasn't left us on our own to figure out dating.

Pray together; then begin video session four.

watch

Use these statements to follow along as you watch video session four.

So you will be delivered from the forbidden woman,
from the adulteress with her smooth words,
who forsakes the companion of her youth
and forgets the covenant of her God.
PROVERBS 2:16-17

A covenant is a binding agreement with another human being under God that says, "I commit all of me to all of you."

Sexuality was never meant to be divorced from intimacy.

The Path to Purity

1. Surround yourself with wise voices.

2. Resist first impulses toward an inappropriate sexuality.

3. Drink from your own cistern.

Such were some of you. But you were washed, you were sanctified,
you were justified in the name of the Lord Jesus Christ.
1 CORINTHIANS 6:11

discuss

Use these questions to discuss the video teaching.

Sex is like a fire. Contained within bricks and steel, fire can bring warmth into the center of a home. Outside those boundaries it brings destruction. In its proper context sex is good and right, bringing warmth to a relationship. Outside its God-intended design, however, sex can bring destruction. The Book of Proverbs was written by a father to his son, who was about to launch into the world.

> **Read Proverbs 2:16-19.**

Ben taught us that sexuality is dangerous when it's divorced from intimacy. Our sexuality is meant to be a component of an integrated experience with another person within the boundaries of marriage, marked by friendship and love.

Ben mentioned that 100 percent of college students surveyed for a study conducted by Notre Dame were casual about sex. Thirty-six percent of college students said their peers were too casual about sex. Forty-one percent said hooking up made them feel disrespected and sad.[5]

> **Ben said sex is the consummation of commitment: all of one person committing to all of another person. In what ways does sex outside marriage cheapen this truth?**

> **Read Proverbs 7:6-27.**

We don't have to go on a hunt for sensuality. Because it's pervasive throughout our culture, it comes looking for us. Sensuality isn't a new, here-and-now problem. It's been around for a long time.

> **How does our culture bombard us with sensuality? Where is it most prevalent?**

Although sensuality bombards us at ever turn and sex is culturally acceptable outside marriage, Ben cited another study stating that teenagers and young adults are having less sex. The main reason? Pornography, the removal of sex from any form of intimacy.[6]

pursuing purity

How has the ease of access to explicit sexual material shaped the view and practice of sex even by people in the church?

The Bible offers healthy ways to cultivate purity in our lives.

1. SURROUND YOURSELF WITH WISE VOICES.

Read Proverbs 6:20. To whom do you turn for wisdom? Whose marriage can you currently look to and say, "I want to be like them in the coming years"?

2. RESIST FIRST IMPULSES TOWARD INAPPROPRIATE SEX.

Ben shared the story of a friend who brought his desktop computer to Ben in order to remove the temptation to view pornography.

How do you personally set guardrails to protect your eyes and your heart from sexual temptation?

3. "DRINK WATER FROM YOUR OWN CISTERN" (PROVERBS 5:15).

Enjoy sex in its right context—marriage. Much of the sexual experience isn't purely biological. God designed sex for our enjoyment.

Growing up, did you view sex as primary good or primarily bad? Who or what influenced your viewpoint?

If you've already committed sexual sin, God offers grace and forgiveness. Cleansing is available through Jesus. If you've experienced Jesus' healing and forgiveness for that kind of sin, describe how you felt.

prayer

Close the session with prayer.

Ask God to help the group evaluate your partners in this season of dating and to guard every step of your journeys. Pray that above all, you'll honor God.

personal study

corinth // biblical case study

Corinth was wild. In fact, before the ancient city of Corinth was destroyed in 146 BC, promiscuity was so rampant that the term "to Corinthianize" could mean "to fornicate," and to call someone a "Corinthian girl" was akin to calling her a whore.[7] Though the city was destroyed and rebuilt anew by the time Paul wrote his letter to Corinth, some of that same reputation remained. As a port city with a lot of money, it could provide travelers with the opportunity for elicit encounters. However, as we've already learned, liberating sexuality from the confines of marriage didn't bring freedom. In fact, one reason the church grew in the earliest days of Christianity is exactly because the sexual ethic of Jesus' followers led to healthier, happier lives, particularly for women.[8]

the issue

Read 1 Corinthians 5:1.

What Paul referred to wasn't just sexual immorality. It had moved well beyond what even the broader culture would condone: a man was sleeping with his stepmother. The Greco-Roman culture of Paul's time was known to tolerate a wide variety of sexual expressions, but even it would have condemned this form of incest. Paul implied that if this behavior was considered shameful by pagans, how much more it should have been condemned by the community of faith.

the excuse and the response

Read 1 Corinthians 5:2.

Church leaders knew the issue persisted, yet they did nothing about it. They didn't confront or condemn, so by their actions they condoned what was happening. Maybe Paul's frustration strikes you as odd until you think more deeply about our modern view of sexuality, even in the church. You've probably heard or said:

pursuing purity

- "This is their issue. It's not hurting me."

- "I'm not going to get involved in their business. What they do with their free time is up to them."

- "Who am I to judge?"

What sorts of problems would issues like persistent sexual immorality have caused in the church at Corinth?

Why was Paul so upset with the Corinthians about this sin?

Paul said the church's failure to confront this sin was rooted in arrogance or pride, and herein we see Paul's larger concern beyond a shameful sin. Their pride had caused them to tolerate practices that grieved the heart of God.

Why do you think Paul connected pride and a failure to confront sin? Has your pride ever kept you from having a difficult conversation with someone?

Why would Paul expect the Corinthians to be filled with grief instead of anger and disgust?

What did Paul mean when he said, "Remove the evil person from among you" (verse 13)? Hint: read verses 9-13 and Jesus' words in Matthew 18:15-17.

Paul didn't tolerate sexual sins, and neither should we. He wasn't flippant and casual about sexual immorality. He didn't make excuses or justify this behavior in the church but confronted members for not being diligent in their fight against sin.

What excuses have you used to justify sinful behavior, especially sexual sins?

What makes these excuses appealing for the people who believe them? Have you ever believed any of them yourself?

If you took 1 Corinthians 5:9 out of context and isolated it as a single verse, what does it seem to advocate?

According to verses 10-11, however, with whom did Paul admonish the Corinthian believers not to associate?

Paul wasn't talking about judging, correcting, and refusing to associate with people outside the faith. He was talking about people who claimed to follow Jesus and whose lives still openly contradicted their faith. Paul told the Corinthians they shouldn't even eat with people who professed faith in Jesus yet, through their actions, mocked their own Savior.

In Paul's day eating was associated with fellowship and community. In that culture it carried much more weight than we might be inclined to give it in a first-pass reading of this text. Paul was warning us against having fellowship with these people.

Where do you currently find biblical community? Why is it essential for those in our Christian community to uphold biblical standards?

According to Paul, what's the difference between someone who has repented of sexual immorality and someone who blatantly continues in their sin? How should we treat both of those people?

the danger

In the previous passages Paul was instructing us in how to treat believers who practice sexual immorality. His next teaching applies on a more personal level.

Read 1 Corinthians 6:12-17.

Paul's words are strong: to practice sexual immorality is akin to joining your body with a prostitute. "But wait! I'm not having sex with a prostitute. I'm just fooling around with my boyfriend/girlfriend." The Corinthians thought because an act was purely physical, it didn't affect their relationship with God. But they were wrong. Paul was saying sexual union affects all we are. Being united with Christ means our whole body is united with Him. Similarly, when we practice sexual immorality, our whole body is united with the other person.

Becoming one spirit with the Lord is great news. Becoming one body with a prostitute is scary news.

If you've ever made a sexual misstep, have you sensed broken fellowship with God? What effect did sexual immorality have on your spiritual life?

the better way

Read 1 Corinthians 6:18-20.

Paul teaches us that the physical union of sexual immorality directly violates our identity as people who've been united with Christ. No other sin carries this consequence. Our bodies were purchased with a price: the death of Jesus. We don't have rights over our own body, much less someone else's. Therefore, Paul tells us to flee sexual sin. Modern culture, like the culture in Corinth, has a casual view of sexuality, but Paul elevated the often unseen yet dangerous consequences.

How is Paul's view of the nature of sexual immorality different from yours?

What lies does our culture teach us about sexual expression in a dating relationship?

Why is sexual purity nonnegotiable for Christians in dating relationships?

The Greek word for "sexual immorality" (verse 18) is the root of our English word *pornography*. It refers to any sexual activity outside the bounds of marriage. We've seen in this study that boyfriend and girlfriend aren't biblical categories. If someone isn't your spouse, they're your brother or your sister in Christ. Our dating lives should be marked by God-honoring purity. That means recognizing that sex is a good gift from a God who loves us, to be enjoyed inside the boundaries of marriage.

However, If you've ever made a sexual mistake, there's hope. Paul didn't leave us with guilt and shame.

Read 1 Corinthians 6:9-11.

pursuing purity

Paul listed a litany of sins, one of which was sexual immorality. People who practice these sins "will not inherit God's kingdom." (verse 9). Paul said some of us were defined by the sins he listed. However, three words give us hope: "used to be" (verse 11). Now we're free from the sins that once had a grip on our hearts. Through Jesus the sin that used to master us has been washed away. Our Savior has justified and sanctified us through the cross.

> **What lies have you told yourself about sexual sins. What truths will you claim from Paul's words?**

It's worth mentioning that in Paul's second letter to the Corinthians, he seems to give us the rest of the story about the guy who was unrepentant of sexually inappropriate behavior. The community confronted him, and he repented. Writing in his follow-up letter, Paul called the Corinthians not only to forgive the man but also to comfort him and love him. God's goal isn't to shame or punish us. On the contrary, a good friend honestly tells you when you're making serious mistakes. The goal is restorative, not punitive. This is good news. If you've been reading this and feel condemned, that isn't the goal. Conviction is, but God convicts us so that He can comfort us. You can change. And the people of Jesus are meant to come around you and support you in the restoration process.

A study of the dangers of sexual immorality can tempt us to think God is antisex, but that's not true. The good news is that God is prosex. Sex was His idea.

> **Read Proverbs 5:18-19.**

It's impossible to "take pleasure in the wife of your youth" (verse 18) and be antisex at the same time. We're encouraged here, in the context of marriage, to have fun. God isn't against sex, but He's against its distortion. Why? Because God is propeople. He's for you and your dating partner. He wants what's best for you because He loves you even more than you love yourself.

Paul's words to the Corinthian church on sexual immorality are strong. Taking time to ask difficult questions of our own hearts to ensure that they line up with the teachings of Scripture is vital if we're going to walk in faith. This section will help us determine whether our hearts and actions conform to biblical truth about sexual purity.

avoid a calloused heart

As we saw in 1 Corinthians 5:1-2, Paul was astonished that the Corinthians weren't grieved over sexual immorality in the church. Sin should cause our hearts to experience grief and anguish because we know we've broken fellowship with our Maker. That's the way our sin affects the heart of God. He grieves when we sin (see Mark 3:1-6).

In what ways have your actions with a current or past dating partner grieved the heart of God?

How have those actions affected your relationship with God?

What can you do right now to reconcile with Him?

When our sin doesn't cause us grief or when we continue sinning in spite of our grief, our hearts begin to grow calloused. To say we have a callous on our hand means a portion of our hand, because of injury, no longer has sensitivity. The callous looks and feels different from the surrounding skin. The same is true of our hearts. When we know right from wrong and good from evil, yet time and time again we choose to feed our sin nature, we repeatedly injure our hearts, and they grow insensitive to God's presence, power, and call. Jesus described this pattern when He quoted the prophet Isaiah in Matthew 13:

> *Isaiah's prophecy is fulfilled in them, which says:*
> *You will listen and listen,*
> *but never understand;*
> *you will look and look,*
> *but never perceive.*
> *For this people's heart has grown callous;*
> *their ears are hard of hearing,*
> *and they have shut their eyes;*
> *otherwise they might see with their eyes,*
> *and hear with their ears, and*
> *understand with their hearts,*
> *and turn back—*
> *and I would heal them.*
> **MATTHEW 13:14-15**

Highlight the actions in the previous verses that had caused the people's hearts to grow calloused.

One of the clearest markers of spiritual growth is an increasing sensitivity to the character and priorities of God. How do you become more sensitive to and aware of God's presence and power in your life?

When was the most recent time you were fully surrendered, through your words and actions, to God's plan and purpose?

a sober warning

Read Ephesians 4:17-24.

In his letter to the Ephesians, Paul warns us of a disturbing reality: we don't simply dwell in disobedience; we advance in it. When we lose sensitivity to God's voice in our lives, we progress further into sensuality and feed an appetite for even greater impurity. What once shocked us now becomes normal. And like many addictions, our growing tolerance means we need more and more to experience the same level of thrill.

Who or what influences your sexual values?

List any people, activities, or ideas that occupy an inordinate amount of time and attention in your life. For hints, check your phone's screen-time usage.

Has a particular sin caused your heart to grow calloused, so that you don't hate and run from it as you once did?

How do we know when our hearts have become calloused? What are the signs?

hope for the hurting

There's hope for a calloused heart, but the battle is tough. Paul's words
are a beacon of light in the darkness: "Some of you used to be like this"
(1 Corinthians 6:11). Paul didn't specify the length of time "used to be" covers.
Maybe "used to be" was years ago. Maybe it was last night. Regardless, "used to be"
is over because we've been "washed … sanctified … justified in the name of the
Lord Jesus Christ and by the Spirit of our God" (verse 11). Elsewhere Paul tells us:

> *There is now no condemnation for those in Christ Jesus.*
> **ROMANS 8:1**

If you're committed to following Jesus and waging war against your sin, the same
can be said of you. Fill in the blanks.

**I used to be known for _____, but now I've been washed
in the name of Jesus.**

I once _____, but now I'm fully clean through Jesus.

The writer of Hebrews said resisting sin can be costly and so painful that it's akin
to shedding blood.

Read Hebrews 12:4.

How did the author of Hebrews describe Jesus' fight against sin?

**What does that description make us realize about our own fight
with sin?**

What has or what will your fight cost you?

If you've made big mistakes before, it's easier to make them again. You experienced consequences, but time has a tendency to numb the effects of sin in your mind if you're not diligent. If you're going to have ongoing victory over sin in your life, you have to surround yourself with people who are headed in the same spiritual direction you want to go.

Read 2 Timothy 2:22.

In a letter to his protégé, Paul told Timothy to run from "youthful passions" and to run toward "righteousness, faith, love, and peace." He encouraged Timothy to do so "along with those who call on the Lord from a pure heart." In other words, pick your tribe wisely.

Read Proverbs 11:14.

If dating is a means of evaluating a potential mate, we should let others offer their wisdom. Romantic feelings are intoxicating and at times can distort our thinking. We need a community of people to serve as guardrails in our lives, helping us continue moving toward Jesus in this season of life.

Who are the people you consider to be your community— the people you've given permission to speak truth into every aspect of your life?

What do you gain from having the perspective of community?

Don't assume people in your community know they're responsible for helping you resist sin and pursue God. They may have no idea you're relying on them. Whether it's a formal small group or just a few friends, let them know you need them for strength, encouragement, and accountability.

What changes about your life when you live as though you're free from condemnation?

How does the freedom from guilt, shame, and condemnation free you to live in a way that pleases God?

If you haven't already done so, begin a conversation this week with someone you trust about your need for ongoing community and counsel in your dating relationship.

NOTES

1. Linda Carroll, "STDs Continue Rapid Rise in U.S., Setting New Record, CDC Says," NBC News, August 28, 2018, https://www.nbcnews.com/health/sexual-health/stds-continue-rapid-rise-u-s-setting-new-record-cdc-n904311.

2. Mark Regnerus, "The Pornographic Double-Bind," First Things, accessed March 11, 2019, https://www.firstthings.com/web-exclusives/2014/11/the-pornographic-double-bind.

3. David Shultz, "Divorce Rates Double When People Start Watching Porn," Science, August 26, 2016, https://www.sciencemag.org/news/2016/08/divorce-rates-double-when-people-start-watching-porn.

4. Brad Porter, "Loneliness Might Be a Bigger Health Risk Than Smoking or Obesity," Forbes, January 18, 2017, https://www.forbes.com/sites/quora/2017/01/18/loneliness-might-be-a-bigger-health-risk-than-smoking-or-obesity/#7f60e2bb25d1.

5. Donna Freitas, "Hookup Culture," Q Ideas, http://qideas.org/videos/hookup-culture/.

6. Kate Julian, "Why Are Young People Having So Little Sex?" The Atlantic, December 2018, https://www.theatlantic.com/magazine/archive/2018/12/the-sex-recession/573949/.

7. D. A. Carson and Douglas J. Moo, An Introduction to the New Testament (Grand Rapids, MI: Zondervan, 2005), 420.

8. Rodney Stark, The Rise of Christianity (Princeton, NJ: Princeton University, 1996), 104.

journal

Though we can't say for certain that all of us will get married someday, imagine that the person you may eventually marry is somewhere out in the world right now. Imagine the community of men and women who currently surround them. Take a moment and describe the way you hope those people would treat your future spouse. How would you like them to behave? What would you hope they would say or refrain from saying? What do you hope they would do or not do?

After you've made a list, ask yourself whether this the way you currently treat the single people around you, who, in all likelihood, are other people's future husbands or wives. You can't control the way the community around your future spouse treats them, but you can control the words and actions you inject into the world. Let your hopes for the community of your future spouse influence the way you treat people around you today.

Use the space provided to record your thoughts.

If we have time

Now that you've finished three sessions on dating, record a plan for your dating season. Use the following questions to get started. If you're engaged or married, focus on what you would have done differently to serve as a guide for others.

What do you want your dating life to look like in practical terms? How will you spend your time as a couple?

What ground rules would you like to establish?

How will you intentionally honor God with everything you are?

session five

engagement

group study

A highs + lows
+ weekend plans
↳ video

Welcome to session five.

How are you practically changing the way you'll date another person, based on last week's study?

How do you determine whether the person you're dating will become the person you marry?

What advice have you received about being certain your boyfriend or girlfriend should be your spouse?

For the past three sessions we've looked at the *who* and the *how* of dating. Now let's explore the next step in the process, one potential conclusion to dating: engagement. This is the season in which two people focus on the complexities of bringing their lives together as one and explore whether this is the one with whom they're going to spend the rest of their lives.

During engagement your single life is passing away, and a new, united life is emerging. Everything is beginning to change as your two lives are becoming one. One of the biggest questions that arise when discussing dating is, How do you know when you know? There's a huge difference between enjoying hanging out with someone and declaring to that person, "I promise to love you in sickness and health until death do us part." How do you know you're ready to get engaged? What should you feel inside? What should you see in your relationship? This session is about engagement. How do you know that you know that you're with the one you should marry? Engagement is about union.

this session's topic

Use this section to provide necessary context for the session's topic.

Engagement is an exciting time filled with activity. At least that's how we're taught to imagine engagement. It's time to plan a wedding—choose a church, flowers, reception venue, photographer, decor, food, who's going to be in the wedding party, right? Your friends and family celebrate you and your fiancé(e) with gifts, showers, and advice. All of these plans are good and helpful, but in the middle of all this activity, you need to remember that engagement is about more than working on a wedding. It's about working on a marriage.

The Bible provides clear direction for knowing whether the person we're with is the right one. The portion of Scripture we'll examine is from one of the most beautiful books in the Bible, a collection of songs written about a man's courtship, wedding, and marriage with his beloved wife. This couple approaches engagement wisely as they grow in their affection for each other and move toward marriage.

As you prepare for marriage, you're planning a wedding. You're beginning to unite your families, your finances, and your futures. You're running into the unknown together. In the midst of all the details, make sure you take time to work on your plans for the marriage itself.

Pray together; then begin video session five.

watch

Signs of a Healthy Relationship

1. Excitement

2. Life

3. A strong sense of commitment

4. The growing skill of communication

5. Surviving a moment of confession

Never assume the other person's motive.

> *Whoever conceals his transgressions will not prosper,*
> *but he who confesses and forsakes them will obtain mercy.*
> **PROVERBS 28:13**

Use these questions to discuss the video teaching.

Ben shared the story of the time he was shopping for an engagement ring for his girlfriend. A conviction rose within him that he was ready to cash in his singleness and be married. From that conviction he provided five indications that your partner is the right person for you long-term.

1. EXCITEMENT. You should feel excitement in your relationship.

> **How excited are you about your relationship right now? What qualities of the other person excite you? If you're married, share what excited you about your spouse as you were dating.**
>
> **Do these aspects of your relationship honor God, and can they stand the test of time?**

Ben identified two aspects of the relationship between Solomon and the Shulamite woman that brought excitement to the relationship: his character and her kindness.

> **Imagine having a child with this person in the future. Are they exhibiting behaviors you'd like to see in your children? Why or why not?**

2. LIFE. Solomon compared his love for his bride to the season of spring.

> **Read Hebrews 10:24. Are you more loving and kind after being around your partner, or are you impatient and bitter? How does your partner spur you on to love and good deeds?**

3. A STRONG SENSE OF COMMITMENT. Solomon noted that death, when it grabs someone, doesn't let go. Our commitment for our partner should be marked by this type of tenacity. A desire to stay is one standard we can use to measure the health of our relationships.

Describe a disagreement you've had in a romantic relationship. What drove you to resolve the disagreement? Share ways you know you're committed to your partner.

What's indicated if you find insufficient desire to resolve conflict?

4. GROWING COMMUNICATION SKILLS. Successful marriages rely on successful communication. These skills should always be honed, but we begin to sharpen them during dating and engagement.

Read Proverbs 12:18. Is your tongue like a sword, or does it bring healing? Be honest with the group.

What makes it so difficult to bring life consistently, day in and day out, with our words?

5. ABILITY TO SURVIVE A MOMENT OF CONFESSION

Read Proverbs 28:13.

When we hide our sins, we don't prosper. We should share all of our heart with someone we hope to marry.

Are there still pieces of your story you haven't shared with your partner? What's keeping you from sharing?

prayer

Close the session with prayer.

Ask God to help the group find excitement about the priorities and pursuits that excite Him. Pray that your commitment won't be rooted simply in physical attraction but always centered on Him through a union forged by His work in your relationships. Commit to being shaped into the image of Jesus as He prepares you for a lifetime together.

personal study

song of solomon // biblical case study

When it comes to young, budding love, the Bible has a great example for us. Beautifully written with symbols and imagery, Song of Solomon is a book that young Jewish boys weren't allowed to read until they were married or adults. It was considered raw and risqué. Reading these first few verses gives us a glimpse into the reason that was the case. This book expounds on the beauties of love in all of its passion, showing us a picture of the kind of love we should aim for as we experience the season of engagement. Song of Solomon shows us how we can have confidence we're with the right person.

excitement

Read Song of Solomon 1:1-4.

"How do I know she's the one?" You may be asking that question right now, and the first answer is found in these verses: excitement.

What in these verses let us know the woman is excited about her man?

"Your name is perfume poured out" (verse 3) is a poetically beautiful way of saying when his name is brought up, it causes a pleasant reaction in her and in others. It's a way of saying that he has a good character. A sweetness. A solid reputation. She's excited to hear his name.

Four people or groups speak in Song of Solomon: God, the man, the woman, and the woman's friends.

Who speaks in the last two lines of these verses? Why does knowing the identity of the speaker matter?

The woman's friends affirm her excitement. Godly love exhibits excitement that's stirred by character and affirmed by others.

What friends do you have with whom to appreciate the ups and downs of a relationship?

friendship

Read Song of Solomon 2:8-10.

Notice the excitement the man has for the woman. He doesn't walk to her. He leaps over the mountains and bounds over the hills. The Hebrew word used in verse 10, translated as "darling," is translated elsewhere in the Old Testament as "neighbor," "companion," or "friend." In other words, their relationship isn't built on physical attraction alone. It's knit closer and closer together by their continued kindness and friendship, which drives the excitement we see in these verses. One biblical mark of a love that lasts a lifetime is friendship.

Why do you think the man and the woman in these verses would prize companionship, not just character?

How do you know you're supposed to be with someone? You want to be with them because there's an ease, not an obligation, in your communication.

growth

Read Song of Solomon 2:11-13. How many references to life and growth do you see in these verses?

What are examples of individual growth that might be evident in a relationship over time?

How do you know you're with the right person? They produce growth in you over time. Different areas of your life begin to blossom and ripen. Because of your relationship with that person, your life begins to look more and more like Jesus. If your life is already growing because of your partner, imagine what it could look like over a lifetime. Conversely, if your partner isn't causing growth in you, imagine the spiritual decline that could occur over a lifetime.

vulnerability

Read Song of Solomon 2:14.

Maybe you, like this couple, have arrived at a place in your relationship where you're increasingly convinced this is the person you're supposed to marry. On the first few dates the risk you took was limited to a little time and money. But as you continued to evaluate each other during the season of dating, the risk increased. The potential of getting hurt grew as you became more vulnerable with each other.

In this verse the man expresses a desire to be with the one he loves. Doves have the ability to make their nest in out-of-the-way places that the casual observer can't see. These words are an invitation to vulnerability and openness.

What's risky about vulnerability?

Have you ever allowed yourself to be vulnerable with someone and gotten burned?

How does vulnerability lay the groundwork for trust?

One way we expose the hidden places of our hearts is through confession. For some of us, that means admitting ways we've been hurt by others in the past. For all of us, it means being honest about ways we've failed to live with purity or integrity. And for all of us, it means being honest about sins we've personally committed. Before you're engaged, you should have weathered a moment of confession between each other. That process continues during engagement. Revealing your missteps during engagement is vital to avoid surprises in marriage and to establish the freedom of knowing all of the doors in your lives are open in your home. This might be a difficult conversation, but wading into these waters signals a deep level of trust in your partner and greatly increases the bond between the two of you.

Vulnerability is a gift that should be reserved for only the strongest relationships. And sometimes we may need a trusted friend or counselor to help us figure out what information and how much detail we should share. Don't let just anyone into the depths of your heart, because once you do, it's impossible to take back what you've divulged. It's in this season of engagement, as your love grows stronger, that you naturally desire more vulnerability from your partner. Whether it's past regrets, insecurities, or heartbreaks, the depths of your heart are hidden from view. Begin praying that when they're revealed to your partner, your voice will be found "sweet" and your face "lovely" (verse 14).

Have you ever thought about reserving this level of emotional vulnerability until engagement? Why or why not?

How is this approach different from the one taken by our culture?

Why might this approach to vulnerability be appealing and helpful?

trust

When vulnerability is received and reciprocated, it allows trust to deepen. The man is extolling the beauty of the inner most places of the woman's heart, the places she may be inclined to hide from view, fearing that if they were exposed, they would leave her raw, ugly, and rejected. The man builds incredible trust by affirming and valuing her as she reveals more and more about herself. How do you know you're supposed to be with someone? You have a relationship marked by trust.

What makes you more or less willing to trust someone else?

How have you expressed a willingness to trust in your relationships?

Trust creates conditions in which love and respect grow and thrive. Yet in any relationship there are impediments that have the potential to stall growth.

Read Song of Solomon 2:15.

Foxes were menaces that ate the buds of the plants in vineyards, thus keeping them from blossoming and becoming fruitful. In Song of Solomon the beloved sees their newfound relationship as a budding vine, and she acknowledges the existence of threats that could severely inhibit their growing love. For this reason she calls on the community to help them identify and eliminate hindrances that could interfere with the growth of their relationship. She instinctively knows that healthy growth will require the aid of a vigilant community.

What are some vulnerabilities for a young couple on the verge of marriage?

How could their community be helpful?

Who are some people you know who are great at helping relationships flourish?

Wisdom is found in community. Some threats are hard for us to see until we've experienced them. Bad communication, inappropriate relationships, poor financial planning, and relationships in each other's family all have the potential to cause stress during engagement. Part of building trust is allowing your community to speak into your relationships from their experience.

The goal of this week's study is to give you confidence to say, "He's the one" or "She's not the one." Let's look at your current engagement or your ideal future relationship and consider whether that love looks anything like the love we find in the Bible.

affection and affirmation

In Song of Solomon 1:3 the woman makes much of the man's name. In comparing it to perfume, she's saying it's pleasing to hear and it awakens something good in her. Don't overlook the value of a good name. Our reputation speaks more about our character than words alone:

A good name is to be chosen over great wealth;
favor is better than silver and gold.
PROVERBS 22:1

Gold and silver in ancient times, as now, were considered two of the most precious, rare materials, of incredible value to those who possessed them. Yet the writer of Proverbs said a good name is more desirable.

How do your actions show that you value your partner's good name more than silver or gold?

What's your internal response when you hear your partner's name?

In Song of Solomon 1 the woman's friends affirmed her excitement. In a season when it's possible for us to be blinded by love, we can learn much from our sober-minded friends who know us and our partner well.

What do your friends say about your partner and their character?

Why should you rely on this insight?

A love worth holding on to is one marked by friendship and kindness. If your partner isn't kind now, putting a ring on their finger and calling them your spouse won't change that. And if your communication feels like an obligation now, getting married won't magically improve your relationship. Throughout Song of Solomon the woman refers to the man as her beloved, conveying the idea of a cherished relationship.

Be honest. Do you cherish the person you're engaged to? Do you get excited when you think about spending time with them?

Is your relationship marked by a natural camaraderie, or does it feel forced? Explain.

As you experience the present and look into the future, you ought to love Jesus and others more because of your partner. Spiritual growth occurs in healthy relationships. Hebrews 10:24 encourages us to "consider"—to spend time thinking creatively and honestly—how we can "stimulate one another to love and good deeds" (NASB). Often we apply "one another" to other church members, neighbors, and coworkers. But what if the primary "one another" in our life is our spouse? You spend plenty of time thinking about wedding plans and date-night plans. Have you put forth the same effort to think about ways you can spur on your partner to love God and others more?

Ask your partner this question and record their answer: "Would you say that because of me, you love God and others more?"

Follow up that question with this one: "How can I more effectively spur you on to love God and others?"

growth and trust

Trust begins to form when you're vulnerable with each other. It's the mark of any healthy relationship. In fact, the Old Testament word most often translated as "trust" also means "careless." This doesn't mean you're flippant and irresponsible. It expresses the idea of a confident, secure attitude, not a guarded, suspicious attitude. You become "careless" because you know whatever piece of your heart is exposed, you're safe, loved, and valued.

What areas of your heart feel the most risky to give away?

How will you know you're ready to trust someone else at a deep level?

Jesus was the purest example of trust. He was trustworthy because He was who He claimed He was, and He did what He claimed He would do. He even encouraged His followers to challenge Him:

> *If I am not doing my Father's works, don't believe me.*
> **JOHN 10:37**

There's a direct correlation between trust and being a person of your word. When you break your word, trust is shattered.

In what ways are you living in a way that fosters trust with your partner?

In what ways is your partner reciprocating?

Confession is one of the deepest ways to build trust. When you can be honest about your past, you open your relationship to a new level of bonding and intimacy. Though wading into these waters is dangerous, it's more dangerous not to confess and to keep your past secrets hidden.

Read Proverbs 28:13. What are the two sides of confession?

If you haven't confessed past sins to your partner, record what you would say.

As we've already observed, increasing emotional transparency builds trust and grows a relationship. Trust and transparency build a foundation on which we can work through problems as they arise. All couples experience issues of some kind. The trust you build during engagement prepares you to work through these challenges with grace and patience.

Each of us communicates differently. Trust is established through healthy communication. How do you like to be communicated with? How does your partner like to be communicated with?

Are you aware of a style of communication that makes you shut down? Why would this be good information to reveal in your relationship?

Do you know of a couple from whom you could gain advice for building trust and open communication in your marriage? What are some questions you would like to ask them?

A relationship characterized by growth and trust is one that can withstand the fiercest storms that life brings its way. You and your betrothed are wise to use your season of engagement to cultivate that kind of relationship.

journal

As you think about uniting your life in marriage with someone else, you'll want to give attention to several key areas. Record what you want your married life to look like in each of the following areas.

What do you want your family to look like when you're a married couple? How do you want people to describe your family?

What will your finances look like? Have you made a budget as a couple? Make a list of financial priorities.

What will your future look like? Sure, nobody can perfectly predict the future, but begin dreaming. Here are a few areas to think about, but don't be limited to these:

Relating to new in-laws: How often do you expect to see them? What happens when you disagree?

Vacation planning: Where? How often? How will you pay for it?

Your preferences or assumptions about housework and chores: Who does what and how often?

Children: How many do you hope to have? What happens if that doesn't go according to your plan?

Any other areas you want to address:

session six

marriage

group study

start

Welcome to session six.

Last week we explored the season of engagement, focusing on the increasing levels of commitment and vulnerability that help you plan your life as a couple. Engagement isn't just about planning a wedding. It's about planning your marriage. Your conversations and experiences during engagement set the stage for the rest of your life together.

> **How have your thoughts on engagement changed as a result of last week's study? How would you answer the question "How do you know that you know?" differently now?**

> **Did your confidence in your relationship change after last week? Are you more or less certain that the person you're with is the one for you?**

> **If you're not in a relationship, what's one takeaway you can apply to your next relationship?**

This week we'll move beyond engagement and into marriage, examining God's design for the most intimate relationship a couple can experience. Marriage reaches its full potential and stands the test of time only when it conforms to the Creator's plan for this life stage.

In this week's study we'll see that God intended marriage to be a picture of Jesus and a pursuit of Him together. A man and a woman form the strongest bonds when they live out their marriage on mission together.

this session's topic

Use this section to provide necessary context for the session's topic.

You've found the one with whom you want to spend the rest of your life. You've dated, evaluated, become engaged, and developed full confidence that this person is the one God designed for you. So now what? How do you live your married life in a way that honors your Creator and each other?

Marriage is a team, a partnership, a union. Whereas God calls singles to uniquely pursue Him as singles, married couples live on mission together. Our marriage will only be as strong as our commitment to each other and to a common set of values. Understanding our unique roles helps us understand how to relate to each other. The problem in many marriages, however, is that this is where the discussion ends. Little work is done to understand what a husband and a wife are to do as they interact with the world as a couple. This week we'll explore what the Bible teaches about marriage as both a picture of Jesus and a pursuit of Him.

Pray together; then begin video session six.

Use these statements to follow along as you watch video session six.

The strongest marriages have a strong commitment to a common mission.

> *Paul left Athens and went to Corinth. And he found a Jew named Aquila,*
> *a native of Pontus, recently come from Italy with his wife Priscilla,*
> *because Claudius had commanded all the Jews to leave Rome.*
> **ACTS 18:1-2**

> *He went to see them, and because he was of the same trade he stayed with*
> *them and worked, for they were tentmakers by trade. And he reasoned in*
> *the synagogue every Sabbath, and tried to persuade Jews and Greeks.*
> **ACTS 18:2-4**

> *And he stayed a year and six months,*
> *teaching the word of God among them.*
> **ACTS 18:11**

> *Show hospitality to one another without grumbling. As each has received*
> *a gift, use it to serve one another, as good stewards of God's varied grace:*
> *whoever speaks, as one who speaks oracles of God; whoever serves,*
> *as one who serves by the strength that God supplies—in order*
> *that in everything God may be glorified through Jesus Christ.*
> **1 PETER 4:9-11**

Marriages on Mission

1. Hospitable

2. Game

3. Faithful

Make the commitment: I exist by Him and for Him, so I will chase Him
till the day I see Him.

Use these questions to discuss the video teaching.

Every human being has two basic desires: belonging and meaning. And the most intimate communities are formed around the deepest causes, whether sports teams, businesses, nonprofits, or marriages. The strongest marriages share a common vision and a common set of values.

What values drive the healthy marriages you've observed?

Ben said, "The strongest marriages have a strong commitment to a common mission."

Have you ever thought about marriage as a means to further the mission of God?

If you're already married, what's your mission together as a couple? If you're not married, what do you hope your common mission will be?

The stronger the vision for your marriage and its mission, the stronger the marriage itself. Three qualities characterize a couple on mission together. Aquila and Priscilla, whom we first meet in Acts 18, embody these qualities.

1. A COUPLE ON MISSION IS HOSPITABLE. As soon as Aquila and Priscilla arrived in their new city, they opened their home to Paul.

How would you define *hospitality*, as demonstrated by Aquila and Priscilla?

According to this definition, are you a hospitable couple?

Aquila and Priscilla leveraged their home and business to help Paul and to tell others about Jesus. What do you have in your life that you could leverage for the same cause? Could your home be a place of ministry? What about your business?

2. A COUPLE ON MISSION IS WILLING SEE THEMSELVES AS A PART OF THE SOLUTION. They seek to be a part of the solution instead of adding to the problem. In Acts 18:24-26 Aquila and Priscilla took the initiative to correct and guide Apollos, a gifted but misguided teacher.

> **Are there needs in your church or community that you find yourself thinking about? Are there ways to serve that God might be putting right in front of you?**
>
> **Are you ready for a challenge in ministry? How do you know?**

3. A COUPLE ON MISSION IS FAITHFUL TO THE END. In 2 Timothy 4:19 Paul mentioned Aquila and Priscilla for the last time in Scripture. Paul encouraged Timothy to greet this hardworking, faithful couple.

> **How do you plan to cultivate active, engaged faith throughout life?**

The couple who lives on mission together experiences indescribable joy and has an impact that lasts throughout eternity.

prayer

Close the session with prayer.

Ask God to help the group be on mission together as couples. Pray that you'll put into practice the lessons you've learned through this study. Submit your lives and relationships to His will, asking Him to teach and bless you through them.

personal study

Marriage is intended to be both a picture of Jesus and a pursuit of Jesus. Scripture provides examples of both, and we find the greatest clarity in the writings of Paul.

submission and sacrifice

Read Ephesians 5:22-24. How did Paul describe the wife's role in marriage?

In what way does a wife's role resemble that of the Church, for whom Jesus died?

Submission isn't subjugation or servitude to all men. It isn't even bowing down to your husband. Submission also doesn't identify you as a second-class person. Rather, submission is an inclination to receive and celebrate a husband's initiation. Often I hear frustration about men's reticence to initiate positive activities for the sake of the family. Many women I know say they would love for a man to initiate date nights, family devotional reading, mission endeavors, or training the kids. Here Paul encourages wives to affirm their husbands' inclinations to lead. It delights the heart of God when His people, the church, receive and affirm his loving actions toward us. In the same way, wives are positioned to breathe encouragement into the hearts of their husbands as they receive and affirm their attempts to lead in a good way.

Now read Ephesians 5:25-33. How does the marriage relationship mirror the relationship between Christ and His Church?

In what ways does a husband's role resemble Jesus' redemptive work?

Husbands are called to love their wives in the same way that Christ loved the church. How did He do it? "He gave Himself up for her." This refers specifically to His death on the cross. While we were sinners, Jesus initiated an act of personal sacrifice so that His bride could be all that she is meant to be under God. This is what men are meant to do. Husbands initiate and sacrifice so that their wives can be fully who they are meant to be under God!

marriage as mission

To live and thrive as a married couple, we're called to leverage our marriage for God's mission. Aquila and Priscilla are beautiful examples.

Read Acts 18:1-2.

The latter half of the Book of Acts focuses primarily on the missionary work of Paul. In this passage we find him in the middle of his second missionary journey, when he met this remarkable couple. In a time when the Jewish population was experiencing much unrest, arguing over whether Jesus was the true Christ, the Roman emperor Claudius had driven the Jews, Aquila and Priscilla among them, out of the city of Rome.

Paul was one of the central figures creating unrest as he worked to spread the gospel. Aquila and Priscilla, driven from their homeland to a city called Corinth, might have been frustrated with Paul. After all, it was because of him they had lost their home. But let's read about their first interaction with Paul.

Read Acts 18:2-4.

Aquila and Priscilla let Paul move in! Paul went out every Sabbath to persuade people that Jesus was the Christ. Then he came back to stay with this couple.

Read Acts 18:11.

Paul didn't just stay with them a couple of nights. He stayed for a year and a half! Remember, Aquila and Priscilla didn't just take in a nice guy who was their friend. Looking back now, thousands of years later, we would gladly welcome the apostle Paul into our home. He literally met Jesus and wrote much of the New Testament. But at this point in history, Aquila and Priscilla were making a risky move. This move, though, made it obvious they were committed to the mission of Jesus, willing to leverage their home and their safety for the advancement of the gospel. Aquila and Priscilla's hospitality is the first characteristic that shows us they were a couple who lived on mission for Jesus.

What initially comes to your mind when you hear the word hospitality?

For Aquila and Priscilla, their home, marriage, business, and everyday lives were centers of ministry. A couple who understands that their marriage is on mission to elevate the name of Jesus will suddenly find that everything they have can be leveraged for the advancement of this great purpose.

What connection do you see between hospitality and God's mission?

What risks were involved in Aquila and Priscilla's hospitality? What do you think it cost them?

When Paul set sail from Corinth to Ephesus, Aquila and Priscilla left with him (see verse 18). When they arrived in Ephesus, Paul left them and returned to Antioch (see verses 19-22). Why did Paul leave them in Ephesus? Apparently, God had other plans for this married couple. While in Ephesus, they met a man named Apollos.

redemptive correction

Read Acts 18:24-25.

Apollos was a talented preacher, and Aquila and Priscilla listened to him teach in the synagogue. Though Apollos was talented, his theology was a bit off in his understanding of Christian baptism.

Have you ever encountered someone whose theology was a bit off track? What did you do?

Read Acts 18:26.

Aquila and Priscilla didn't complain to others in the synagogue about Apollos's poor theology. They didn't post a video online to shame him. They didn't whisper behind his back. They also didn't wait for Paul or another pastor to arrive and correct him. "They took him aside" without humiliation or public shame, correcting him in a redemptive, edifying way. Their words served to build him up rather than tear him down. Why did they approach Apollos this way? Because their primary concern as a couple was for the gospel to go forth with integrity and power.

Have you ever confronted someone about an error in doctrine? How did it go?

Have you ever been confronted for correction? How did it go?

Not only were Aquila and Priscilla willing to leverage their home and business for the sake of the gospel, but they also saw every situation as an opportunity for ministry. They took great ownership and care in God's mission, so they couldn't let doctrinal error stand. Instead, they lovingly corrected Apollos. This couple embodied living on mission.

In the past year what problems have arisen in your Christian community that gave you opportunities to serve the body rather than be a part of the problem?

Read Acts 18:27-28.

Aquila and Priscilla's redemptive approach to correction meant Apollos would go on to have an incredible gospel ministry. Paul later mentioned him in 1 Corinthians 3:6-8, placing their ministries on the same level. Through Aquila and Priscilla's loving influence, Apollos could continue being a force for the gospel of Jesus Christ.

In what ways would you like your marriage to be like the ministry of Aquila and Priscilla?

continue in shared ministry

We don't see Aquila and Priscilla in the narrative of Acts again, but Paul mentioned them again in three of his letters.

Read 1 Corinthians 16:19.

Paul closed his letter to the church in Corinth by naming Aquila and Priscilla, who had joined his work there. Aquila and Priscilla's ministry of hospitality continued, and apparently, their tent-making business was lucrative enough that the church could meet in their home.

In what ways could your home be an extension of your ministry to the local church?

Aquila and Priscilla appeared again a few years later in the conclusion of Paul's letter to the Romans.

Read Romans 16:3-5. What did Paul thank them for?

Did you notice that Priscilla's name is spelled differently? This isn't a typo. It's the more formal pronunciation of her name, signifying Paul's desire to sound official in stating her name. He viewed her as an equal partner. She worked hard for the sake of the gospel.

Paul also said Aquila and Priscilla "risked their own necks" (verse 4) for him. Though we can't be sure when and how this event happened, it points to their faithfulness to Paul and God's mission despite dangerous circumstances.

In the final letter of Paul we have on record, 2 Timothy, he again concluded with a mention of Aquila and Priscilla.

Read 2 Timothy 4:6-8,19.

In a letter that had nothing to do with this couple, what's the significance of this mention in a letter written from prison near the end of Paul's life?

Timothy was Paul's protégé, and Aquila and Priscilla were serving alongside him, shoulder to shoulder. This was disciple making in action. In short, this couple was faithful. Through major life moves and in the face of danger, Aquila and Priscilla model for us the truth that even through seasons of change, we never have to change our mission for God.

Aquila and Priscilla, though culturally and linguistically far removed from our current lives, are a shining example of a healthy marriage. The way they approached faith together is still relevant today. The questions we'll consider in this section don't center on whether relevancy remains but on whether our marriage looks anything like the one we've read about in Scripture.

the model marriage

Ephesians 5 details the roles of husbands and wives and the ways they're to relate to each other. None of us will ever be perfect, an exact picture of Jesus and His church. But that's the picture we strive for.

Wives, what are some positive decisions or habits in your husband's life that you can affirm and celebrate?

Husbands, what are some ways you can take the initiative to encourage your wife?

Wives, what are some things you wish your husband would do? How could you encourage him to lead in a way that builds him up rather than shames him?

Husbands, what are some sacrificial decisions you could make in order to use your time, money, and resources to help your wife grow as a woman of God?

hospitality

Aquila and Priscilla took a risk in expressing hospitality. This wasn't a casual dinner club they were hosting. It was dangerous financially, physically, and spiritually.

Are you being risky in ministering through hospitality? What risks do you face?

What has your hospitality cost you in this season, or what could it cost you in seasons to come?

Have you ever physically relocated to a new area as a couple, as Aquila and Priscilla did? What challenges did you face?

If you haven't made a move like that, review Acts 18 and record the actions Aquila and Priscilla took that gave purpose to their move and to their life as a married couple, despite changing circumstances.

Read 1 Peter 4:9-11.

Verse 10 gives us another perspective on hospitality, beyond the physical act of being hospitable in our actions. It delves into the motivations and attitudes of the heart. The goal of hospitality isn't simply an action but a heart that serves others without grumbling, whining, and complaining.

If someone peered into your heart, not just your actions, would they say you express hospitality "without complaining" (v. 9)?

As a couple, have you grumbled about an act of hospitality, either before or after the act? What effect did that have on the act itself?

common mission

You may be inclined to think you can't have a ministry impact unless you're a preacher because preachers do the real work of ministry. But as we read in 1 Peter 4:10-11, that assumption couldn't be further from the truth. This passage emphasizes that you can use whatever gifts God has given you to serve others.

How are you, as a couple, using your gifts to generously bless and serve others?

How does it feel to receive hospitality when someone else uses their gifts to serve you?

Another part of living on mission is to see every moment as an opportunity for ministry. That's what Aquila and Priscilla did as they served Paul despite difficult circumstances; as they served Apollos despite an awkward, difficult confrontation; and as they hosted the early church. They were living out Paul's words to the Ephesians:

> *We are his workmanship, created in Christ Jesus for good works, which God prepared ahead of time for us to do.*
> **EPHESIANS 2:10**

Do you truly believe you're God's handiwork? Do you truly believe your spouse is God's handiwork as well?

How should this truth affect your relationship, especially during disagreements?

Paul said we're created for good works. When we marry someone who was also created for good works, our ministry potential multiplies.

What good works are you and your spouse currently doing in this season?

How could ministering with your spouse to meet needs in your community lead you to go outside your comfort zone?

Knowing that making a meaningful impact might bring discomfort to one or both of you, how can you agree on a common mission and continue to support each other?

faithfulness

When we talk about faithfulness in marriage, the discussion tends to revolve around faithfulness to each other as a couple. But faithfulness to the gospel and to your mission together is also important.

In his letter to the Romans, Paul thanked Aquila and Priscilla (see 16:3-5). At this point in your marriage, would someone else thank you for your faithfulness in ministry?

If not, what are some changes you could make?

investment

Someone invested in you to bring you to a point of ministry impact today. They were your Paul and Apollos, watering the seeds of the gospel in your life.

Read 1 Corinthians 3:6. Just as someone helped you knew Jesus better, you have the opportunity to make Him known to others Whom are you watering as Apollos watered the Corinthians?

What does watering as a couple look like?

Priscilla worked hard for the sake of the gospel. In Colossians 3:23-24 Paul urges us to work at everything with all of our hearts, as if we were working for the Lord. These verses apply to the work we do as married couples to advance the gospel.

Read Colossians 3:23-24. How would someone describe your effort to advance the gospel of Jesus?

How is this effort stretching you? How is it exciting you?

Aquila and Priscilla demonstrate that the Christian life is one of continual investment. Marriages are another avenue to make disciples who make disciples.

In whom are you investing your life?

How are you growing personally as you invest in others?

journal

Congratulations! You've reached the end of our study. Our hope is that as you've leaned in and considered the unique purposes of singleness, dating, engagement, and marriage, you've allowed Scripture to deepen your understanding and fortify your commitment to live God's best in whatever relational stage you're in. In this final journal section, take some time to evaluate your journey.

As you've walked through this study, how have your beliefs and assumptions about singleness, dating, engagement, and marriage been challenged?

What has God done in your heart as you've thought about these ideas during the past six sessions?

What would you say is your one key takeaway from this study?

How will that takeaway help you advise and counsel friends who are experiencing different relational stages?

leader's guide

prepare to lead
Watch the session's teaching video and read the group content with the leader's guide in hand to understand how it supplements each section of the group study.

big picture
Use this section to help focus your preparation and leadership during the group session. Take note of the highlighted points.

cultural versus biblical
Most people have been taught to think about the issues in this study by our culture, not by the church. The point of this study is to help participants think biblically about different relational stages. This section, along with "This Session's Topic" in each group session, should provide assistance in leading from a biblical framework.

considerations
Because most people have experience with singleness, dating, engagement, and marriage, this section alerts you to some of the assumptions members may bring with them to the group sessions.

pray
Pray for group members as part of your preparation to lead each session. Brief sample prayers are provided.

tips for leading a small group

Follow these guidelines to prepare for each session.

prayerfully prepare

REVIEW. Review the personal studies and group questions ahead of time.

PRAY. Be intentional about praying for each person in the group. Ask the Holy Spirit to work through you and the group discussion as you point to Jesus each week through God's Word.

minimize distractions

Create a comfortable environment. If group members are uncomfortable, they'll be distracted and therefore not engaged in the group experience. Plan ahead by considering these details:

Seating

Temperature

Lighting

Food or drink

Surrounding noise

General cleanliness

At best, thoughtfulness and hospitality show guests and group members they're welcome and valued in whatever environment you choose to gather. At worst, people may never notice your effort, but they're also not distracted. Do everything in your ability to help people focus on what's most important: connecting with God, with the Bible, and with one another.

include others

Your goal is to foster a community in which people are welcome just as they are but encouraged to grow spiritually. Always be aware of opportunities to include any people who visit the group and to invite new people to join your group. An inexpensive way to make first-time guests feel welcome or to invite someone to get involved is to give them their own copies of this Bible-study book.

encourage discussion

A good small-group experience has the following characteristics.

EVERYONE PARTICIPATES. Encourage everyone to ask questions, share responses, or read aloud.

NO ONE DOMINATES—NOT EVEN THE LEADER. Be sure that your time speaking as a leader takes up less than half of your time together as a group. Politely guide discussion if anyone dominates.

NOBODY IS RUSHED THROUGH QUESTIONS. Don't feel that a moment of silence is a bad thing. People often need time to think about their responses to questions they've just heard or to gain courage to share what God is stirring in their hearts.

INPUT IS AFFIRMED AND FOLLOWED UP. Make sure you point out something true or helpful in a response. Don't just move on. Build community with follow-up questions, asking how other people have experienced similar things or how a truth has shaped their understanding of God and the Scripture you're studying. People are less likely to speak up if they fear that you don't actually want to hear their answers or that you're looking for only a certain answer.

GOD AND HIS WORD ARE CENTRAL. Opinions and experiences can be helpful, but God has given us the truth. Trust God's Word to be the authority and God's Spirit to work in people's lives. You can't change anyone, but God can. Continually point people to the Word and to active steps of faith.

session one

big picture

Singleness isn't just a second-class phase of life we rush through. Singleness affords opportunities, and God has purpose for this season. We shouldn't miss what He wants to teach us now because we're fixated on the future.

In the season of singleness, we find freedom we won't experience in subsequent phases of life.

1. FREEDOM FROM DISTRACTION. In other stages of life, it's easy to be distracted by the opposite sex instead of focusing on unhindered devotion to God.

2. FREEDOM FROM ANXIETY. We'll have divided interests in other seasons of life. Singleness gives us freedom from the anxieties and stresses of a relationship.

cultural versus biblical

Our culture tends to view singleness in one of two ways: a time to relish and work on ourselves or a phase of life to be terminated as quickly as possible. Both views miss the mark biblically.

Help members of your group see the unique gift and opportunity singleness provides to live fully on mission for God. Singleness shouldn't be leveraged to focus exclusively on ourselves or our career but on our unique calling and role in the work God is doing in the world.

considerations

In any group of singles, there will likely be a range of people—some who are content in their singleness and others who are discontent. Neither is inherently wrong. Regardless of where someone falls on the spectrum, data suggest that most people who are single hope to be married eventually. Help both groups realize that the purpose of this stage is to pursue Christ with purity of devotion.

As the leader, uphold singleness in the same positive light the Bible does. Singleness is a good gift from a God who loves us, not an unfortunate stage to be endured.

pray

God, we want to see singleness the same way You do. We want to use this time to make the most of our calling and the most of Your kingdom. Please help the people in this group, no matter how we feel about being single, become more committed to You with unwavering devotion. Use this Bible study to deepen our faith and to point us to You and Your purpose for our lives.

notes

session two

big picture

Dating is a process of evaluation, and that process begins with finding who to date. The goal of this session isn't to discover how to find a date but to identify what type of people you should date. To determine this, Ben suggests that you seek someone with the following characteristics.

- Someone who has the same **cause** as you

- Someone who has **character** shaped by God

- Someone with whom you share **chemistry**

cultural versus biblical

In a culture dominated by a consumer mentality, especially in regard to dating, followers of Christ aim for much more. Society bases relationships on transient characteristics, such as physical looks, which will fade over time. This emphasis dehumanizes people. Scripture calls us first to place our allegiance in God. As we maintain that allegiance throughout a dating relationship, we should focus on character and chemistry. To pursue only one of these three qualities is to miss God's best for us.

Though we'd like to create categories of boyfriend and girlfriend, the goal of dating is to answer the question, Is this person the right one for me?

considerations

Ben mentions in his talk that the Bible doesn't recognize the categories boyfriend and girlfriend. This statement is likely news to many people in your group and may even be news to you. Most of us tend to reject information that goes against our experience. Resist this urge and hear Ben's point. The idea of evaluating a mate is very much a biblical concept. The goal of this session is to apply those biblical principles to dating.

Members of your group may be dating people without the same cause, character shaped by God, or chemistry. All three elements are needed. Be aware that this teaching may present a difficult but needed realization for some members.

This session emphasizes the importance of meeting people to date in the context of Christian community. Many people find dates through less personal platforms like dating apps. Although nothing is inherently wrong with those, help the group see the value of a shared Christian community as a means to meet other people.

pray

> *God, let us prize and seek relationships with people of character and faith. The people we date will shape our lives and character over time, and we want to date people who push our faith to greater depths. Lord, help us desire to be the type of couple who build each other's faith. Please lead us in this process.*

notes

session three

big picture

The Bible doesn't contain a how-to guide for dating, because dating isn't a biblical concept. However, the evaluation of a potential mate is wholly biblical. This session will give members some practical criteria for what dating should look like, bringing much-needed clarity to the process of dating.

As we date, we want to date with clarity and autonomy.

1. CLARITY. We're up-front and direct about how we feel and what we think throughout the process.

2. AUTONOMY. We don't use our dating status to lay claim on someone's time or body. The Bible allows for neither option.

cultural versus biblical

It's nearly impossible to avoid being influenced by the way culture approaches dating. However, asking the question "How does God want me to date?" can help make the period of dating even more fulfilling in both the short and long terms.

In dating, culture and intuition may not provide helpful guidance, although we've been trained to think they will. Scripture provides that guidance. The Bible never uses the terms *boyfriend* and *girlfriend,* a status our culture often assigns to designate a sense of ownership over another person. The Bible gives two categories of relationship: we're either single or married. Until we're married, we have no rights over another person.

When we date, starting in the right place is key. If we want to find someone who's seeking God, we have to look where people seek Him. Because dating is a season devoted to evaluating the other person, offering clarity about our thoughts and feelings is a sign of maturity and integrity.

To evaluate, we have to watch and learn. Through observation in multiple environments, we find out whether the other person is truly who we think they are.

considerations

When people approach the topic of how to date, they have lots of presuppositions and assumptions. There will likely be as many opinions about dating as their are people in your group. You'll want to account for that possibility in your conversation.

Much of how we think about dating is cultural rather than biblical. Just because a person's friends date a certain way doesn't make it wise or biblical. Here are a few examples of people you may need to consider.

1. **MISSIONARY DATERS.** Some Christians date someone who doesn't share their faith in the hopes they'll convert them. Though this may seem like a good idea, it's a path to heartbreak. Shared faith is an essential component of healthy relationships.

2. **CLAIM STAKERS.** Others may use the terms *boyfriend* and *girlfriend* to lay claim to someone. In dating, however, we need space to evaluate whether the person is right for us.

3. **SERIAL MONOGAMISTS.** The goal of dating is marriage. Jumping from person to person with no clear goal or end in sight doesn't meet the biblical standard for our relationships.

pray

God, we want to honor You in this season of evaluation, but we need You to help us see what You see in the people we date. Help us discern the true character of our dating partners. Give us clarity and courage to speak openly and honestly. Keep us from rushing ahead of You or lagging behind. Help us stay in step with You as You lead us through this process.

session four

big picture

In this second half of our approach to dating, we'll look at the process itself. The culture surrounding us takes a casual view of sex. We hear that sex is essential to our well-being, whether or not we're married. And society claims that sex is primarily physical, with no significant effects on our mind or spirit.

In his talk Ben offers three ideas for pursuing purity.

1. **SURROUND YOURSELF WITH WISE VOICES.** Whom we listen to and speak with about dating matters, especially in regard to purity.

2. **RESIST FIRST IMPULSES TOWARD INAPPROPRIATE SEX.** Sexual temptation abounds. The quickest and surest way out is to "flee sexual immorality" (1 Corinthians 6:18).

3. **"DRINK WATER FROM YOUR OWN CISTERN" (PROVERBS 5:15).** Sex is permissible only within the confines of marriage.

cultural versus biblical

Our world of casual sex tells us in order to evaluate whether someone is the right person and in order to be physically healthy, we must sleep together. The Bible calls us to something different. The truths of Scripture stand in stark contrast to what pop culture and relational self-help books esteem as wisdom.

Scripture carves another pathway for our thoughts and actions. The Bible calls us to purity, choosing love over lust. We should treat the other person graciously, as if we were dating a child of royalty. We should always surround ourselves with a community of people who know our strengths, weaknesses, hopes, dreams, and desires and who choose to remain present and active with us during this phase.

considerations

The pathway of purity is fraught with challenges, but for those who've already sinned sexually, God offers grace. If someone in the group has sinned and feels a weight of guilt, be sure not to add guilt and shame. Help them understand that they can be forgiven and can begin pursuing purity from this day forward despite past failings.

Additionally, pornography usage is rampant. Purity isn't simply what happens between two people; it may be what happens between someone and their computer. It's possible that members of your group have struggled with pornography in the past or are struggling now. Maybe you've personally struggled in this area.

The people in your group need to know they can pursue purity and find freedom from sexual sin. The purpose of this session isn't to heap condemnation but to help people maintain freedom from sexual impurity.

pray

God, we want to be people who desire purity at all costs. Help us reject cultural expectations and see our dating partners as brothert or sisters in Christ. Help us fight the battle for purity, which is too difficult to fight on our own. Help us support one another in this pursuit. We believe You're able to give us victory.

notes

session five

big picture

Dating is a process that culminates in marriage. How do we know we should marry the person we're dating? This session aims to answer that question and then to establish steps to take after we've made that initial decision. Engagement is the time when we bare our hearts and seriously consider what it means to become one with another person.

Ben teaches in his talk that we can know the person is right for us if we find the following qualities in the relationship.

1. EXCITEMENT. We should feel excitement in the relationship.

2. LIFE. Solomon compared his love for his bride to the season of spring.

3. A STRONG SENSE OF COMMITMENT. A desire to stay is one standard we can use to measure the health of our relationship.

4. GROWING COMMUNICATION SKILLS. Successful marriages rely on successful communication. These skills should always be honed, but we begin to sharpen them during dating and engagement.

5. ABILITY TO SURVIVE A MOMENT OF CONFESSION. Marriage is hard. We need to be honest.

cultural versus biblical

Engagement in our culture is all about wedding planning. We ask: What dress and tux should we wear? What should the flowers look like? Who'll be in the wedding party? Where will we live after we're married? Biblically, engagement is a brief season that allows a couple to focus on the complexities of bringing their two lives together as one. It's is not only a time to work on the wedding but also a time to work on the marriage. Engagement involves wedding planning, but it's primarily about union.

considerations

Help members see that engagement is the final step in evaluating a mate. Although it should be exciting, it should also be a time of serious consideration. The couple is beginning to knit their lives together.

Engaged couples are often surprised to learn how stressful engagement can be, so don't be surprised if engaged couples in your group express that sentiment.

Urge engaged members to seek premarital counseling. Many churches provide some form of this with either a pastor or a counselor. Having an objective party to advise and encourage the couple during this season is tremendously helpful.

pray

> *God, we want to see each stage of our relationships as You do. Please craft our relationships in such a way that the current or eventual engagements of the people in this group will exalt You. Allow this group session to be helpful and productive for them.*

notes

session six

big picture

Just as God called us when we were single to pursue Him uniquely in that phase, He has also called us to pursue Him uniquely as a married couple. Marriage is a about couples being on mission.

1. A COUPLE ON MISSION IS HOSPITABLE. They extend grace and help others walk with the Lord.

2. A COUPLE ON MISSION IS WILLING TO TRY SOMETHING NEW. They seek ways to advance God's kingdom.

3. A COUPLE ON MISSION IS FAITHFUL TO THE END. Faithfulness continues at every point in the marriage.

cultural versus biblical

Marriage in our culture is disposable and can be ended by the choice of either party at any moment. Such ideas of marriage fall woefully short of the biblical ideal. Biblical marriage has a twofold design.

1. A PICTURE OF JESUS AND HIS RELATIONSHIP WITH HIS BRIDE, THE CHURCH. Wives are to submit to their husbands, and husbands are to initiate and lead. When these roles work in harmony, marriage can provide a beautiful picture of Jesus and His church.

2. A PURSUIT OF GOD'S MISSION. Through hospitality, ministry, and faithfulness to each other and God's call, marriage is more than a couple who lives as one. Marriage involves pursuing God's mission together. The strongest bonds are formed when a couple lives out their marriage on mission together.

considerations

Hopefully, this session will be an exciting conclusion to your study together. Here are a couple of points to keep in mind.

1. EXPERIENCE WITH MARRIAGE. Our experience with marriage colors our expectations of marriage. It's likely that some people in the group have never seen a godly marriage, so the biblical ideal will be new to them.

2. EXPERIENCE WITH DIVORCE. Other members may have divorced parents or may have been divorced themselves and are now single again. Be aware of the experiences these members might bring to the discussion. Help them feel comfortable.

pray

God, we want marriages that last and that point others to You. Give us marriages that picture the reality of Your relationship with Your church. Strengthen the marriages in our church and in our community so that they honor You and reflect Your purpose.

notes

more from
ben stuart

Continue your journey through the
4 stages of relationship in Ben Stuart's
book, *Single. Dating. Engaged. Married.*

W PUBLISHING GROUP
AN IMPRINT OF THOMAS NELSON

The Jesus Bible

sixty-six books. one story. all about one name

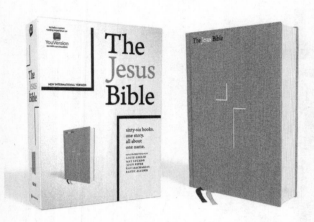

The Jesus Bible, NIV & ESV editions, with feature essays from Louie Giglio, Max Lucado, John Piper, and Randy Alcorn, as well as profound yet accessible study features will help you meet Jesus throughout Scripture

- 350 full page articles
- 700 side-bar articles
- Book introductions
- Room for journaling

The Jesus Bible Journal, NIV
Study individual books of the Bible featuring lined journal space and commentary from *The Jesus Bible.*

- 14 journals covering 30 books of the Bible
- 2 boxed sets (OT & NT)

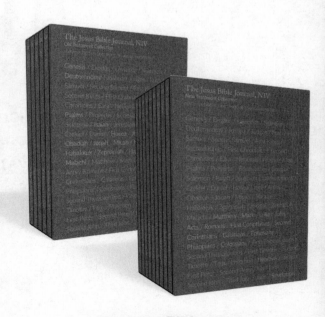

TheJesusBible.com